Jesus The Muslim Prophet

History Speaks of a Human Messiah Not a Divine Christ

Louay Fatoohi

Luna Plena Publishing   Birmingham

© 2010 Louay Fatoohi

All Rights reserved. No part of this book may be reproduced, translated, stored in a retrieval system, or transmitted by any means, electronic, mechanical, photocopying, recording, or otherwise, without written permission from the author.

Scripture quotations are from The Holy Bible, English Standard Version®, copyright © 2001 by Crossway Bibles, a publishing ministry of Good News Publishers. Used by permission. All rights reserved.

Production Reference: 1260110

First published: February 2010

Published by:
Luna Plena Publishing
Birmingham, UK.
www.lunaplenapub.com

ISBN 978-1-906342-07-4

Cover design by:
Mawlid Design
www.mawliddesign.com

Cover image:
Created by the cover designer, the arabesque encompasses Jesus' Arabic name, titles, and attributes in the Qur'an. It is surrounded with translations of most of these titles, as well as the significant expression "son of man" which Jesus is found applying to himself over 80 times in the Gospels.

About the Author

Louay Fatoohi is a British scholar who was born in Baghdad, Iraq, in 1961. He converted from Christianity to Islam in his early twenties. He obtained a BSc in Physics from the College of Sciences, University of Baghdad, in 1984. He received a PhD in Astronomy from the Physics Department, Durham University, in 1998.

The author of several books and over forty scientific and general articles in Arabic and English, Dr Fatoohi is particularly interested in studying historical characters and events that are mentioned in the Qur'an and comparing the Qur'anic account with the Biblical narratives, other Jewish and Christian writings, and historical sources. His most recent books are:

- *Jihad in the Qur'an: The Truth from the Source.*
- *The Mystery of the Messiah: The Messiahship of Jesus in the Qur'an, New Testament, Old Testament, and Other Sources.*
- *The Mystery of the Crucifixion: The Attempt to Kill Jesus in the Qur'an, the New Testament, and Historical Sources.*
- *The Mystery of Israel in Ancient Egypt: The Exodus in the Qur'an, the Old Testament, Archaeological Finds, and Historical Sources.*
- *The Mystery of the Historical Jesus: The Messiah in the Qur'an, the Bible, and Historical Sources.*
- *The Prophet Joseph in the Qur'an, the Bible, and History: A new detailed commentary on the Qur'anic Chapter of Joseph.*

Contents

Preface 1
Introduction 3

Part I: The Muslim Jesus 7
1. Muslim Messenger and Prophet 9
Islam 9
Jesus the Prophet 12
Jesus the Messenger 14
The Human Nature of the Prophets 16
"Prophet" Jesus in the Gospels 20
Jesus' Mission 23

2. The Human Historical Messiah 29
The Human Jewish Messiah 29
The Divine Christ 30
The Human Masīh of the Qur'an 31

Part II: "Son of Mary" Not "Son of God" 33
3. The Non-Divine Jewish "Sonship of God" 35

4. The Christian "Sonship of God" 39
Christian Sons of God 39
The Unique Son of God 41
The Eternal Son of John 45
When Did Jesus' Sonship of God become Special? 48
Sonship of God, Messiahship, and Miracle Working 52
Sonship of God and Blasphemy 53

5. The Qur'an's Rejection of the "Sonship of God" 57
The Oneness of God 57
No Offspring of God 59
Jesus' False "Sonship of God" 63

6. Son of Man 73
The Unhistorical Link Between "Son of Man" and "Messiah" 73
Jesus' Use of the Term "Son of Man" 78

Part III: A Divine Theology for a Non-Divine Jesus 85
7. Pauline Christianity 87
Paul's Unhistorical Jesus 87
The Doctrine of the Atonement 92
Johannine Theology: The Ultimate Fruit of Pauline Christianity 93
The Heterogeneous Scriptural Sources of Christianity 95

8. The Trinity 99

　　　　The Development of the Doctrine of the Trinity 100
　　　　The Fallacy of the Trinity 103
9. Jesus: A Man Created by God and a God Created by Humans 107

Appendix A. The Qur'anic Verses that Refute Jesus' Divinity 111

References 115

Index of Qur'anic Verses 117

Index of Biblical Passages 120

Index of Names and Subjects 123

Preface

Like my books *The Mystery of the Messiah* (2009) and *The Mystery of the Crucifixion* (2008), this book is derived from parts of my comprehensive book *The Mystery of the Historical Jesus: The Messiah in the Qur'an, the Bible, and Historical Sources* (2007). The latter is a broad study of Jesus' life and teachings, whereas the derivative works each focuses on and studies in more detail a specific aspect of the history of Jesus.

This book is based mainly on two chapters — "The Divine Son of God That Jesus Never Was" and "The Human Jesus" — from my book on the historical Jesus, as well as some material from my other writings. I have also expanded the study significantly with new material. Furthermore, I have changed the structure of the borrowed content for a better presentation, which was also necessary to incorporate the new material.

Like my other writings, this book tries to bring the Qur'an to the study of the historical Jesus which Western scholarship has mainly restricted to the Old and New Testaments, along with historical writings. My other, related goal is to get Islamic scholarship to show more interest in historical sources and to also look at the Old and New Testaments and other Jewish and Christian sources from a historical perspective.

This book focuses on contrasting the human Jesus of the Qur'an with the divine Jesus of Christian sources. Admittedly, this subject has been examined by Christian, Muslim, and other scholars considerably more than other topics of the historical Jesus. However, one new contribution to the literature that my book makes is to show that the human Jesus as presented in the Qur'an is the one that fits in history. The concept of a divine Jesus can only be an invention from the post-Jesus era.

This book, as is the case with all of my other works, has been significantly improved by the insightful comments and feedback of my dear wife Shetha Al-Dargazelli. Without Shetha's support, it would have been very difficult for me to write my books.

The book has also benefited from the careful reading and comments of my ever helpful friend Tariq Chaudhry.

Introduction

Whether Jesus was a man or a god and man at the same time is one fundamental theological difference between Islam and Christianity. The Qur'an presents Jesus as a prophet of Islam, the one religion that all of God's prophets from Adam to Muhammad preached. All Muslim prophets were human with no divine qualities, and so was Jesus. While the Qur'an says that God conferred so much favour on Jesus, it stresses that he was a mere mortal human being. It states that there was, is, and will always be one God. Christian sources, on the other hand, present Jesus as a man yet also elevate him to divinity.

The Gospels, other New Testament books, and Christian apocryphal writings make statements about Jesus that can only mean he was like any human being. For instance, Jesus is described as a "prophet" (e.g. Mark 6:2-5), "rabbi" (e.g. Mark 9:5), and even "servant" of God (e.g. Matt. 12:17-18). Yet the same sources contain passages that describe him in terms that can only mean that he was divine. For instance, Paul (Phi. 2:6) states that Jesus was "in the form of God." Paul and other New Testament authors believed in the doctrine of Incarnation, which states that God descended as a human being in the form of Jesus. Most of the passages that deify Jesus also talk about his relation with God in a way that suggests that they are two separate beings, yet other passages confuse the two and all but remove any distinction between them. This, for instance, is what John (10:30) does when he makes Jesus declare: "I and the Father are one."

This confusing language is not the result, as Christians believe, of Jesus' complex nature. After all, there is no point in trying to use a human language to describe something that it is not equipped to do. The simple explanation of this confusion is that those different passages were written over a long period of time by different people who held irreconcilable beliefs. Not even any one Gospel is an authentic piece of work by any one man. It is a compilation of different traditions that the author gathered and to which he added his own views. Jesus' appearance did not represent a shift in the concept of salvation. Otherwise, the coming of the one and only man-God would have meant that the billions who lived before him were unfairly denied the grace of the new salvation. The fact is that God did not change how He deals with man. It was, rather, some people who changed the truth about Jesus and succeeded in popularizing their unhistorical beliefs about him.

The confused relationship between God and Jesus has resulted in the development of competing Christian theological concepts to describe this unique relationship. For instance, some theologians, like John, believed that Jesus was divine from eternity. Adoptionists, on the other hand, claim that Jesus became divine at some point in his life. When this exactly happened is itself a point of disagreement among adoptionists.

How can someone be a god and man at the same time? Docetism tried to tackle this question by claiming that Jesus had only an appearance and did not have a physical body. Jesus did not suffer on the cross, Docetists argued, because he was god and did not have a body. Everything that happened to Jesus' body, including the crucifixion, was an illusion. Others considered Docetism as sheer heresy.

The nature of the god-man unity that Jesus represented became a battleground for competing articulations of this concept — a concept that was unheard of in monotheism. The history of the development of the doctrine of Trinity, which I discuss in the book, epitomizes the struggle of theologians to cope with what sounds more like a logical fallacy than a meaningful concept.

Leaving aside the logical problems in any expression of a man-god unity, this book will try and show that history also rejects the suggestion that it was Jesus who taught that he had a divine nature. In fact, we will see how he put the efforts to preempt what he knew was going to happen after him, stressing that he was the "son of man" not the "son of God."

The book has three parts consisting of 9 chapters and 1 appendix. **Part I** focuses on the historical, human Jesus and consists of two chapters. **Chapter 1** presents the image of Jesus in the Qur'an. It first introduces the Qur'anic concepts of "Islam" and "prophethood" before explaining how Jesus is described as a Muslim prophet. This identity means that he was human not divine. The chapter then shows that Jesus' image as a "prophet" is also found in the Gospels.

Both the Qur'an and Christian sources accept Jesus as the Messiah. Judaism also has the concept of the Messiah, but the Jews reject the identification of Jesus with the Messiah and argue that the latter is yet to come. **Chapter 2** highlights the significant similarity between Judaism and Islam in that both religions consider the Messiah a human being. It also contrasts this image of the Messiah with its Christian counterpart which presents the Christ as divine.

The remaining two parts of the book focus on history's rejection of the suggestion that Jesus was divine. This false divinity is what stops most Christians from seeing Jesus how he really was: a Muslim prophet.

Part II, which consists of four chapters, examines in detail the various forms of the concept of "son of God." **Chapter 3** shows that Jewish sources used the expression "sonship of God" figuratively. It did not suggest any form of divinity. The very different application of the concept of "son of God" to Jesus in Christian sources is discussed in **Chapter 4**. It also shows differences between the New Testament authors' presentations of Jesus' sonship of God. The Qur'anic rejection of Jesus' sonship of God is the focus of **Chapter 5**. The expression "son of man," which is found mainly in the Gospels in the New Testament, is highly significant for this discussion and is the subject of **Chapter 6**.

The last three chapters of the book make up **Part III**. This part looks at how Jesus was transformed into a divine individual by some of his followers, shows the historical and logical problems in this image, and discusses its refutation in the Qur'an. **Chapter 7** explains how Paul developed the divine Jesus, thus playing a bigger role than Jesus himself in defining Christianity. It also discusses how the image of Jesus in the Gospel of John became the prevailing image in Christianity, despite its substantial difference with his image in the other Gospels. The Johannine image of Jesus removes any distinction between Jesus and God. Finally, the chapter explains a fundamental difference between the Qur'an and the Christian scriptures.

Chapter 8 studies one of the most important doctrines of Christianity and which is completely based on Jesus' divine image: the Trinity. The chapter explains this doctrine, how it developed, and how it is rejected in the Qur'an. The last chapter of this part and the book, **Chapter 9**, draws on the previous 8 chapters to show how Jesus' human image was changed over time to turn him from the human, Muslim prophet he claimed to be into a divine being that the apostle Paul and others who did not see or know Jesus preached. Naturally, his teachings were accordingly distorted to reflect his alleged divine nature.

For easy reference, I have compiled in **Appendix A** all Qur'anic verses that *explicitly* reject the divinity of Jesus.

For the reader's convenience, the book has three indexes for the Qur'anic verses, Biblical passages, and names and subjects.

The book uses a number of styles. Each Qur'anic verse has been followed by a combination of two numbers identifying its *sūra* or "chapter" and its position in that chapter. For instance, the combination 3.59 refers to the 59th verse of the 3rd chapter.

The translations of the Qur'anic verses are mine. Translation is an act of interpretation and therefore reflects the translator's understanding of the text. This is why I always use my own translations of the Qur'an, even though I usually consult some existing English translations.

Square brackets have been used to enclose explanatory texts that are needed to clarify the translation. Alternative texts, such as the English meaning of a term that is quoted in its Arabic origin, are enclosed in parentheses.

All Biblical quotation are from the *English Standard Version* (ESV) Bible. First published in 2001, this modern translation is partly based on the *King James Version*.

The book uses a number of different printing styles. Different fonts have been used for the text, Qur'anic verses, and Biblical passages. Roman transliterations of Arabic terms are in italics.

Finally, readers' feedback is welcome at fatoohi_louay@gmail.com. Readers are also welcome to visit my website www.quranicstudies.com for more of my writings.

Part I

The Muslim Jesus

1. Muslim Messenger and Prophet 9
   Islam.. 9
   Jesus the Prophet..12
   Jesus the Messenger...14
   The Human Nature of the Prophets...16
   "Prophet" Jesus in the Gospels...20
   Jesus' Mission..23
2. The Human Historical Messiah..29
   The Human Jewish Messiah 29
   The Divine Christ..30
   The Human Masīh of the Qur'an 31

He (Jesus) said: "I am Allah's servant. He has given me the Book and has made me a prophet."

(Qur'an, 19.30)

1

Muslim Messenger and Prophet

The Qur'an considers Jesus a man. He was not God or a god. He had no divine quality. He is portrayed in the Qur'an as a *prophet of Islam*. This description might sound rather odd to those who are not familiar with the Qur'anic meaning of Islam and think that it is the religion that is associated with Prophet Muhammad only. We will, therefore, first look at the concept of "Islam" in the Qur'an before we discuss the image of Jesus as a Muslim prophet and messenger.

Islam

The Arabic verb *yuslim* means "to surrender" or "to submit." It is used in a special way in the Qur'an to mean *to surrender (one's self) to God*. The derived Qur'anic noun *Islām*, thus, means *surrender or submission to God*. To be a Muslim is to believe in God, whom the Qur'an calls "Allah," as the One Lord, submit to His will, and carry out His commandments.

Contrary to the common misconception that it is the religion that was revealed to Prophet Muhammad only, Islam is the name of the universal religion that God commanded, through His various messengers, all people to embrace.

The Qur'an tells us that the name "Muslim" was in fact coined by God who used it long before Prophet Muhammad and the Qur'an:

> Do jihad [O you who believe!] in the way of Allah the kind of jihad that is due to Him. He has chosen you and has not laid upon you a hardship in religion; it is the faith of your father Abraham. He [Allah] has named you *al-Muslimīn* (the Muslims) earlier and in this (the Qur'an), so that the Messenger be a witness over you, and you be witnesses over people. Therefore keep up prayer, pay the obligatory alms, and hold fast to Allah. He is your Master; so how excellent a Master and how excellent a Supporter! (22.78)

God has named the followers of His religion "Muslims" not only in the Qur'an but also in books that He revealed to previous prophets, such as the Torah of Moses and the Injīl of Jesus.

The following verse states that prophet Noah, who lived long before prophet Abraham, told his people that God ordered him to be "one of the Muslims":

> But if you [O people!] turn away [from my call], I have not asked you for any reward; my reward is only with Allah, and I have been commanded to be one of the Muslims. (10.72)

Thus, previous divine books and prophets used terms equivalent to "Islam" and "Muslim" in their respective languages.

Islam is the name of the one religion that Allah, the One and only God, revealed to every prophet He sent to people since the first man and prophet, Adam. For instance, all of the following prophets were Muslims who taught Islam to people: Noah, Abraham, Ishmael, Isaac, Jacob, Joseph, Moses, Aaron, David, Solomon, Zechariah, John, and Jesus. The following verse describes Israelite prophets as "Muslims":

> Surely We revealed the Torah in which there was guidance and light; with it, the prophets who became Muslims judged for the Jews. (5.44)

These are other verses about prophets Abraham and his sons and grandsons:

> And who turns away from the religion of Abraham but he who makes himself a fool; and surely We chose him (Abraham) in this world, and in the hereafter he is surely among the righteous. (2.130) When his Lord said to him: "Be a Muslim"; he said: "I have become a Muslim (I have submitted) to the Lord of the people." (2.131) And Abraham enjoined the same on his sons, and so did Jacob (Abraham's grandson): "O my sons! Surely Allah has chosen for you the [true] religion, therefore die not except as Muslims." (2.132) Or were you [O People of the Book!] witnesses when death visited Jacob, when he said to his sons: "What will you worship after me?" They said: "We shall worship your God and the God of your fathers Abraham, Ishmael and Isaac, [who is] one God, and to Him we are Muslims (submit)." (2.133)

Significantly, Muhammad's followers are usually called "those who believe," in reference to the fact that they believed in Muhammad. Another term that is used much less is "believers." Clearly, the term "Muslim" is universal and not restricted to those who followed Muhammad. Here is another instructive observation: even when naming specific religious groups, such as the Jews and Christians, the Qur'an never identifies the followers of Muhammad as "Muslims" as a way to differentiate them from the other groups. The Prophet's followers are called "those who believe," as in the following verse:

> Those who believe, the Jews, the Christians, and the Sabaeans — whoever believe in Allah and the Last day and does good — they shall

have their reward from their Lord, and there is no fear for them, nor shall they grieve. (2.62)

The commissioning of Muhammad was not an unprecedented or unique event. It was another instance of God sending a prophet, which is how He communicated with people:

Say [O Muhammad!]: "I am not a novelty among the messengers, nor do I know what will be done with me or with you. I only follow that which is revealed to me; I am but a manifest warner [of hell]." (46.9)

The revelation that Muhammad received came from the same source of the earlier divine revelations:

We have revealed to you [O Muhammad!] as we revealed to Noah and the prophets after him; and as We revealed to Abraham, Ishmael, Isaac, Jacob, the children of Jacob, Jesus, Job, Jonah, Aaron, and Solomon. And We gave David a Book. (4.163) And [We gave revelations] to other messengers whom We have mentioned to you before and other messengers whom We have not mentioned to you. And Allah spoke to Moses — certainly spoke to him. (4.164)

He has ordained for you [O you who believe!] the religion that He enjoined on Noah; that which We revealed to you [O Muhammad!]; and that which We enjoined on Abraham, Moses, and Jesus: "Establish the religion, and make no divisions therein." What you call the polytheists to is hard for them. Allah chooses for Himself whom He wills, and guides to Him who turns to Him. (42.13)

Muhammad's message was a continuation of the previous messages, in the same way that Jesus' message continued on from Moses', Moses' message continued on from Joseph's, Joseph's continued on from Jacob's, and so on. All messengers taught the same creeds, such as the oneness of God. But their teachings had some different practices and behavioral codes, which were also commanded by God. These reflected cultural differences between the societies to which they were sent, were intended to respond to certain events, or were simply tests for the believers. As we shall see later, Jesus made lawful some foods that had been declared unlawful by the Mosaic law (p. 23).

What distinguishes Prophet Muhammad from other Muslim prophets is that he is the *last prophet* of Islam, which means that the Qur'an is the last divine Book:

[O people!] Muhammad is not the father of any of your men, but he is the Messenger of Allah and the last of the prophets; and Allah is aware of everything. (33.40)

In addition to the belief in the oneness of God, the hereafter, and the angels, the Qur'an requires the Muslim to believe in all previous messengers and the books and messages that God revealed to them. This is consistent with the Qur'an's affirmation that all messengers taught the same religion and were sent by the one and same God. The Muslim is commanded to hold all prophets in high esteem and reverence. The failure to believe in any prophet is a failure to believe in all prophets, and a failure to be a Muslim:

> The Messenger [Muhammad] believes in that which has been revealed to him from his Lord, and so do the believers; they all believe in Allah, His angels, His Books, and His messengers; we do not discriminate between any of His messengers; and they say: "We hear and obey [Allah's commandments]; grant us Your forgiveness, our Lord. And to You is the eventual course." (2.285)

This brief introduction should help in understanding the Qur'an's description of Jesus as a Muslim prophet.

Jesus the Prophet

The Arabic word for "prophet" is *nabī*, whose root is *naba'*, which means "news" or "tidings." The word for "prophecy" is *nubū'a* and is derived from the same root. A "prophet" in the Qur'an is a *human being* to whom God revealed tidings of the Day of Resurrection and religious teachings. The prophet is charged with communicating this knowledge to people so that they may know the purpose of their creation and live as God wants. As we have already seen, Biblical figures such as Adam, Solomon, David, Moses, Zechariah, John, and many others were all prophets.

Jesus, the Qur'an tells us, was a prophet (also 4.163):

> He (Jesus) said: "I am Allah's servant. He has given me the Book and has made me a prophet." (19.30)

> And when We took a covenant from the prophets; and from you [O Muhammad!]; and from Noah, Abraham, Moses, and Jesus son of Mary. We took from them a solemn covenant. (33.7)

The following verse also confirms the prophethood of Jesus, but in the context of reminding the Jews, Christians, and Muslims that they must believe in all prophets and equally honor them (also 3.84):

> Say [O you who believe!]: "We believe in Allah; in that which has been sent down to us; in that which was sent down to Abraham, Ishmael, Isaac, Jacob, and the children of Jacob; in that which was given to Moses

and Jesus; and in that which was given to the prophets from their Lord. We do not discriminate between any of them, and to Him we are Muslims (we submit)." (2.136)

As all prophets were Muslims and taught Islam, their true followers were also called Muslims. These two verses show that Jesus' companions called themselves Muslims:

> But when Jesus perceived disbelief on their (the Children of Israel's) part, he said: "Who are my supporters in the cause of Allah?" The companions said: "We are Allah's supporters. We believe in Allah, and do you bear witness that we are Muslims." (3.52)
>
> Lo! When I inspired the companions: "Believe in Me and in My messenger (Jesus)." They said: "We believe. Bear witness that we are Muslims." (5.111)

Jesus was one of the prophets, but he was also distinguished and, in some aspects, unique. He is the only prophet who did not have a biological father. Probably related to his unique miraculous conception is his other distinctive quality that he became a prophet while still in his mother's womb or immediately after his birth. This is what the infant Jesus said to his mother's people in defense of her chastity when, upon returning to them carrying her newborn, they suspected that she had conceived Jesus illegitimately: "I am Allah's servant. He has given me the Book and has made me a prophet" (19.30). Jesus' unique conception and the fact that, unlike other prophets, he was made a prophet immediately after his birth, or even while still in his mother's womb, must have distinguished him with special spiritual qualities.

Believing in every prophet is an essential requirement of Islam, because all prophets had one and the same message. This duty does not mean that all prophets have the same spiritual status. God mentions in a number of verses that He privileged some prophets more than others. For instance, some prophets were given more knowledge, others were given scriptures, and so on:

> Your Lord [O Muhammad!] best knows those who are in the heavens and the earth. We conferred on some prophets more favor than others, and We gave David a Book. (17.55)

In another verse that states that God endowed some prophets with more gifts than others, Jesus is singled out as one of those specially favored prophets:

> Those are the messengers. We conferred on some more favor than others. Among them there are some to whom Allah spoke, while some of them He exalted [above others] in degree; and We gave Jesus son of Mary clear proofs and supported him with the Spirit of Holiness (Gabriel). (2.253)

God here emphasize two major favors that He bestowed on Jesus but not on many other prophets: the ability to perform miracles and the support with Gabriel. Although Gabriel delivered the Qur'an to Prophet Muhammad and probably communicated with other prophets, only Jesus is described as having been "supported" by Gabriel — probably hinting at a unique role that Gabriel played in Jesus' life. This should not be surprising given that, according to the Qur'an, Gabriel was also involved in the miraculous conception of Jesus, not only conveyed the news about it. As I have explained elsewhere, Gabriel's visit was conducive and essential to the occurrence of that miracle of non-sexual conception (Fatoohi, 2007: 90-97).

With respect to miracles, the Qur'an tells us that other prophets were also given the gift of performing miracles. The verse above contrasts Jesus with other prophets who did not work wonders, but it may also imply that Jesus performed more miracles than the prophets who did. This may also be concluded from the mention of Jesus' miracles in some detail in a number of verses. These are the kind of miracles that the Qur'an says Jesus performed:

(1) Speaking in infancy.
(2) Showing paranormal precociousness in infancy.
(3) Creating figures of birds from clay and then giving them life.
(4) Healing blindness.
(5) Healing albinism or serious skin diseases.
(6) Raising the dead.
(7) Knowing what people ate and stored in the privacy of their homes.
(8) Bringing down from heaven a table of food.

Jesus the Messenger

Another Qur'anic term related to "prophet" is "messenger." The latter has a broader sense, denoting anyone that God sends on a mission, such as delivering a message or performing a particular task.

As a prophet is sent by God to deliver a message to people, every prophet is a messenger. But the opposite is not true. Not every messenger is a prophet, because not every messenger receives from God the kind of knowledge that characterizes prophethood — that is, knowledge of religion and the Day of Judgment — or is charged with the responsibility of acting as a religious teacher to people. Also, unlike the title "prophet" which is applied to human beings only, "messenger" is a title that is used in the Qur'an for non-humans also, such as angels.

Many Muslim scholars have taken the opposite view, thinking that messengers are a special group of prophets whose messages are targeted at a larger number of people than other prophets. There are observations from the Qur'an that refute this view. **First**, the Qur'an uses the title "messenger" for some prophets, such as Hūd (7.67), whose preaching activities and influence were limited in place and time and could not be compared to those of other prophets, such as Moses and Muhammad, whose messages spread far and survived well beyond their times.

Second, the angels, who are spiritual beings, and who are never called "prophets," are called "messengers," because they are *sent* by God to people on specific missions:

> Praise be to Allah, who has created the heavens and the earth, and who has made the angels messengers. (35.1)

The angels who were sent to prophets Abraham and Lot (11.69-83, 15.51-74, 29.31-34), those who attend the dying person (6.61, 7.37), and those who record what people say and do (43.80) are all called "messengers," but not prophets:

> He is triumphant over His servants. He sends recorders over you, until when anyone of you is visited by death, Our messengers take him and they do not neglect [their duties]. (6.61)

> Or do they think that We do not hear their secret and their private talk? Yes, and Our messengers are present with them writing down. (43.80)

Third, the Qur'an uses the title "messenger" several times to denote *any* human spiritual guide inspired and sent to people by God, without any other specific attributes, such as targeting a larger number of people:

> We did not send any messenger but that he should be obeyed by Allah's permission. (4.64)

Four, a prophet is a human being but a messenger may or may not be a human being. The following verse indicates that prophets were all human beings, so the term "messenger," which is applied to the angels also, cannot be included in the term "prophet":

> And We have not sent [prophets] before you [O Muhammad!] but men to whom We gave revelations, [who were] from the people of the towns. (12.109)

So prophets are a special category of messengers, not the other way around.

Being a prophet, Jesus is naturally described as a "messenger" also:

> We gave Moses the Book and followed him with a succession of messengers. And We gave Jesus son of Mary clear proofs, and We supported him with the Spirit of Holiness. Is it that whenever a messenger came to you [O Children of Israel!] with what you did not like you grew arrogant, some you disbelieved and some you killed? (2.87)

> And [He shall make him] a messenger to the Children of Israel. (3.49)

> The Messiah son of Mary was no other than a messenger before whom [similar] messengers passed away. (5.75)

> Then We made Our messengers to follow in their (Noah and Abraham) footsteps, and followed them up with Jesus son of Mary. (57.27)

So Jesus is explicitly described as a "messenger" and "prophet" in the Qur'an.

The Human Nature of the Prophets

The Qur'an is absolutely clear that all those it describes as prophets were human beings. Even though their lives may have involved some miracles, they lived like every human being. They needed food and drink, worked, fell ill, got married, and so on.

As we explained earlier, prophets were sent by God, so they were also messengers. Yet the polytheistic population of Arabia, and many other peoples and cultures, believed that any individual sent by God or a god must be divine in some way. But as all prophets were known to be human beings to their peoples, their human nature became one argument used by the disbelievers to reject their claims as messengers sent by God.

The Qur'an mentions a number of prophets who had to defend themselves against the claim that since they were human beings, they could not have been God's messengers. They include Noah (11.27,

23.24), Ṣāliḥ (26.154, 54.24), Shu'ayb (26.186), Moses and Aaron (23.47), and Muhammad (17.94, 21.3).

In the following verses, God explains that messengers who were sent to teach human beings religion had to be humans themselves, and that had the population of the earth been angels, His messengers to them would also have been angels:

> And nothing prevented people from believing when the guidance came to them except that they said: "What! Has Allah sent a human being to be a messenger?" (17.94) Say [O Muhammad!]: "Had there been on earth angels walking about feeling secure, We would certainly have sent down to them from the heaven an angel as a messenger." (17.95)

For instance, when prophet Ṣāliḥ was sent to his people, they rejected him, with one reason being that they could not believe that, being human like them, he could have received revelation from God. Even if they could accept that God may have chosen a human being as a messenger, they argued, they could not believe that it could have been Ṣāliḥ:

> The [people of] Thamūd rejected their warnings. (54.23) They said: "A human being from among ourselves that we are to follow? In that case we would be in delusion and madness. (54.24) Has the Remembrance been sent down to him from among us? He must be an insolent liar." (54.25)

The following verses show a typical exchange between prophets and their disbelieving people where the former argue that they could not come up with miracles at will, to satisfy their doubting people, as they were mere human beings who could perform miracles only when God allows this:

> Their messengers said: "Is there a doubt about Allah, the Creator of the heavens and the earth? It is He who invites you, in order that He may forgive you your sins and give you respite until an appointed term." They said: "You are no more than human beings, like us! You wish to turn us away from what our fathers used to worship; bring us then some clear authority." (14.10) Their messengers said to them: "True, we are human beings like you, but Allah confers His favor on such of his servants as He pleases. It is not for us to bring you an authority except as Allah permits. And on Allah let all believers rely." (14.11)

Like all other prophets, Jesus was a human being. The Qur'an tells us that Jesus stressed his human nature in his teachings and that his deification was the result of changes made to his original message after him by some of his followers. Jesus told people that he was God's servant and prophet, and that he also had to worship God like he was calling them to do:

> I am Allah's *servant*. He has given me the Book and has made me a *prophet*. (19.30) He has made me blessed wherever I may be. He has enjoined upon me prayer and almsgiving so long as I remain alive. (19.31)

I should note that the Arabic term *'abd*, which I have translated as "servant," means "slave" also. It is used in the Qur'an to indicate the total submission and servitude of the created to the Creator.

Significantly, the New Testament also describes Jesus as a "servant." This title is used once for Jesus in the Gospels:

> This was to fulfill what was spoken by the prophet Isaiah: "Behold, my *servant* whom I have chosen, my beloved with whom my soul is well pleased. I will put my Spirit upon him, and he will proclaim justice to the Gentiles." (Matt. 12:17-18)

In the Book of Acts, the title "servant" of God is used for Jesus twice by Peter after he healed a crippled man (also Acts 3:26):

> The God of Abraham, the God of Isaac, and the God of Jacob, the God of our fathers, glorified his *servant* Jesus, whom you delivered over and denied in the presence of Pilate, when he had decided to release him. (Acts 3:13)

Peter and John twice call Jesus God's "servant" after they were released by the Sanhedrin (also Acts 4:30):

> For truly in this city there were gathered together against your holy *servant* Jesus, whom you anointed, both Herod and Pontius Pilate, along with the Gentiles and the peoples of Israel. (Acts 4:27)

But, of course, the New Testament also promotes Jesus' divinity. Describing Jesus as both "servant" of God and "divine" is another aspect of Jesus' confused nature in the New Testament. It looks even more so when one notes that Jesus himself is reported to have clearly differentiated between the servant and his master in several parables and sayings, such as this:

> A disciple is not above his teacher, nor a servant above his master. It is enough for the disciple to be like his teacher, and the servant like his master. (Matt. 10:24-25)

This Pauline passage is one clear example of Jesus' confused nature in the New Testament:

> Have this mind among yourselves, which is yours in Christ Jesus, who, though he was in the form of God, did not count equality with God a

thing to be grasped, but made himself nothing, taking the form of a servant, being born in the likeness of men. And being found in human form, he humbled himself by becoming obedient to the point of death, even death on a cross. (Phi. 2:5-8)

In the Qur'an, servanthood is a description of the created, whereas lordship and divinity are exclusive descriptions of the Creator. The Qur'anic term *'abd* (servant or slave) does not apply to Jesus only, but to all created beings.

Jesus asked people to obey him, because he was a trustworthy messenger of God — his and everybody else's Lord:

> Keep your duty to Allah, and obey me. (43.63) Allah is my Lord and your Lord. So worship Him. This is a straight way. (43.64)

The Qur'an stresses that Jesus' unique, miraculous conception did not mean that he was not a human being. He was a miraculously created human being like the first human being:

> The likeness of Jesus in Allah's eye is as the likeness of Adam. He created him of dust, then He said to him "Be!" and he is. (3.59)

Note also the emphasis in this verse that Jesus was created of dust like all human beings (22.5, 30.20). I have discussed in detail elsewhere the nature of the miraculous creation of Jesus as a human being (Fatoohi, 2007: 99-119).

In the New Testament, Paul also makes a link between Jesus and Adam, but one that is completely different from the Qur'an's. He links the two through his doctrine of Atonement. He explains that because Adam sinned, all his descendants inherited this sin which causes death. Through his resurrection, Jesus can free people from their sins and give them eternal life. After describing Jesus as a second Adam who gives life, Paul goes on to talk about the creation of the two:

> Thus it is written, "The first man Adam became a living being"; the last Adam became a life-giving spirit. But it is not the spiritual that is first but the natural, and then the spiritual. The first man was from the earth, a man of dust; the second man is from heaven. As was the man of dust, so also are those who are of the dust, and as is the man of heaven, so also are those who are of heaven. Just as we have borne the image of the man of dust, we shall also bear the image of the man of heaven. I tell you this, brothers: flesh and blood cannot inherit the kingdom of God, nor does the perishable inherit the imperishable. (1 Cor. 15:45-50)

What Paul says, as he stresses that Jesus and Adam were of completely different natures, is the exact opposite to the Qur'an's statement which confirms the similarity between the creation of Adam and Jesus as being both from dust. Paul has stated in another epistle that Jesus "was descended from David according to the flesh" (Rom. 1:3), clearly indicating that Jesus had another, deeper reality than his human body.

Paul's misguided comparison between Jesus and Adam looks to me a "contextual displacement" of the authentic comparison between the two that God must have made in the book that He revealed to Jesus and/or which Jesus himself spoke of, which is repeated in the Qur'an. I have coined the term "contextual displacement" to refer to a special kind of textual corruption in Jewish and Christian writings where "a character, event, or statement appears in one context in the Qur'an and in a different context in other sources." Contextual displacements are the results of "the Bible's editors moving figures, events, and statements from their correct, original contexts" (Fatoohi, 2007: 39).

"Prophet" Jesus in the Gospels

One title that the New Testament gives to Jesus is "prophet," using it in its Old Testament sense. A prophet in the Old Testament is someone who has had a revelation from God and speaks for Him. What is significant about the fact that the New Testament calls Jesus a "prophet" is that this title is used in the Old Testament, and accordingly in the New Testament, for human beings only. Judaism does not accept that anyone other than God, including prophets, can have divine attributes anyway.

Significantly, the Gospels tell us that not only people called Jesus a "prophet," but he also used this title for himself. In one instance, Jesus complained that a prophet is mistreated in his hometown and by his family and relatives, in a clear reference to how he was treated by people (also Matt. 13:55-58; Luke 4:22-24; John 4:44):

> And on the Sabbath he began to teach in the synagogue, and many who heard him were astonished, saying, "Where did this man get these things? What is the wisdom given to him? How are such mighty works done by his hands? Is not this the carpenter, the son of Mary and brother of James and Joses and Judas and Simon? And are not his sisters here with us?" And they took offense at him. And Jesus said to them, "A prophet is not without honor, except in his hometown and among his relatives and in his

own household." And he could do no mighty work there, except that he laid his hands on a few sick people and healed them. (Mark 6:2-5)

In this dialog with his disciples also Jesus likens himself to a prophet:

Whoever receives you receives me, and whoever receives me receives him who sent me. The one who receives a prophet because he is a prophet will receive a prophet's reward, and the one who receives a righteous person because he is a righteous person will receive a righteous person's reward. (Matt. 10:40-41)

Luke reports a third incident in which Jesus called himself a prophet:

At that very hour some Pharisees came and said to him, "Get away from here, for Herod wants to kill you." And he said to them, "Go and tell that fox, 'Behold, I cast out demons and perform cures today and tomorrow, and the third day I finish my course. Nevertheless, I must go on my way today and tomorrow and the day following, for it cannot be that a prophet should perish away from Jerusalem.' O Jerusalem, Jerusalem, the city that kills the prophets and stones those who are sent to it! How often would I have gathered your children together as a hen gathers her brood under her wings, and you would not! (Luke 13:31-34)

Jesus' disciples also called him a "prophet," as in this dialog with two of them who did not realize that they were speaking to Jesus after his resurrection:

Then one of them, named Cleopas, answered him, "Are you the only visitor to Jerusalem who does not know the things that have happened there in these days?" And he said to them, "What things?" And they said to him, "Concerning Jesus of Nazareth, a man who was a prophet mighty in deed and word before God and all the people." (Luke 24:18-19)

Peter is also reported to have identified the prophet whose coming was predicted by Moses with Jesus:

That times of refreshing may come from the presence of the Lord, and that he may send the Christ appointed for you, Jesus, whom heaven must receive until the time for restoring all the things about which God spoke by the mouth of his holy prophets long ago. Moses said, "The Lord God will raise up for you a prophet like me from your brothers. You shall listen to him in whatever he tells you." (Acts 3:20-22)

This passage is from the Book of Acts, so not only the Gospels call Jesus a "prophet." The prophecy of Moses that is quoted above is from Deuteronomy 18:15.

People also thought that Jesus was a "prophet." This is one

incident in which people speculated that Jesus was a prophet (also Matt. 16:13-14; Luke 9:18-19):

> And Jesus went on with his disciples to the villages of Caesarea Philippi. And on the way he asked his disciples, "Who do people say that I am?" And they told him, "John the Baptist; and others say, Elijah; and others, one of the prophets." (Mark 8:27-28)

A similar uncertainty about what prophet Jesus was is reported by Mark and Luke (9:7-8):

> King Herod heard of it, for Jesus' name had become known. Some said, "John the Baptist has been raised from the dead. That is why these miraculous powers are at work in him." But others said, "He is Elijah." And others said, "He is a prophet, like one of the prophets of old." (Mark 6:14-15)

There are several incidents in which people declared with certainty that Jesus was a prophet, and some of these are quoted below:

> And when he entered Jerusalem, the whole city was stirred up, saying, "Who is this?" And the crowds said, "This is the prophet Jesus, from Nazareth of Galilee." (Matt. 21:10-11)

> And although they were seeking to arrest him, they feared the crowds, because they held him to be a prophet. (Matt. 21:46)

> Then he came up and touched the bier, and the bearers stood still. And he said, "Young man, I say to you, arise." And the dead man sat up and began to speak, and Jesus gave him to his mother. Fear seized them all, and they glorified God, saying, "A great prophet has arisen among us!" and "God has visited his people!" (Luke 7:14-16)

> Now when the Pharisee who had invited him saw this, he said to himself, "If this man were a prophet, he would have known who and what sort of woman this is who is touching him, for she is a sinner." (Luke 7:39)

Interestingly, even the Gospel of John which, as we will later see, differs from the Synoptics in clearly treating Jesus as a god from eternity reports a number of incidents in which people called Jesus a prophet (John 4:17-19, 6:12-14, 7:39-40, 7:50-52, 9:16-17).

All these references point to how Jesus introduced himself and how he was seen by people: a prophet sent by God. This is how he is presented in the Qur'an. Jesus' divine image is a later development that the historical Jesus had no hand in and even forewarned against, as we shall see later.

I should mention that other titles that confirm Jesus' human nature are also applied to him in the Gospels. One particularly significant title is "servant," which was discussed earlier (p. 18). Another title that clearly implies that Jesus was a human being is "rabbi" or "teacher" (e.g. Mark 9:5; Matt. 26:25).

Jesus' Mission

All messengers called people to the way of God, carrying the same divine message. Each also confirmed the verity of the messengers sent before him. Naturally, Jesus was also given these responsibilities, confirming the verity of Moses' book, the Torah, and reminding people of their duties to God:

> I have come to confirm that which was revealed before me of the Torah, and to make lawful some of that which was forbidden to you. I have come to you with a sign from your Lord, so keep your duty to Allah and obey me. (3.50)

Certain prophets were also given other, specific duties. For instance, Abraham was commanded to build the Ka'ba and establish the ritual of pilgrimage (2.127-128, 22.26-27). Moses was charged with the responsibility of taking the Israelites out of Egypt (e.g. 20.47). In the case of Jesus, one such responsibility was to modify the Mosaic law by legalizing some things that had been unlawful to the Jews. The divine law may be divided into two parts that may be described as *doctrinal* and *behavioral*. The doctrinal law covers various fundamental beliefs, such as the oneness of God, the worship-worthiness of God only, and necessity of the belief in all of His messengers and their divine books. This part of the law never changed. Conversely, the behavioral part of the law, which covers various practices, rituals, and codes of conduct, may be changed.

Verse 3.50 does not detail what unlawful things Jesus made lawful. These most probably included foods, but they are also likely to have included other things. Had it been food or any one type of thing only, the verse would probably have named it. The wording of the verse suggests that Jesus was commanded to relax the law of the Torah on a number of different things. This relaxation of the Mosaic law is likely to have been included in Jesus' book, the Injīl, as shown in this verse that states that, like the Torah, the Injīl had to be observed:

> If they (the People of the Book) had observed the Torah, the Injīl, and that which was sent down to them from their Lord, they would have been nourished from above them and from beneath their feet. There is a

moderate nation among them, but many of them follow an evil course. (5.66)

Jesus' book complemented the book that the Jews already had. Interestingly, the Gospel of Matthew also confirms that Jesus' message was a continuation of the law, as seen in this passage and the six "antitheses" that follow it in his sermon to his disciples on the mountain:

> Do not think that I have come to abolish the Law or the Prophets; I have not come to abolish them but to fulfill them. For truly, I say to you, until heaven and earth pass away, not an iota, not a dot, will pass from the Law until all is accomplished. Therefore whoever relaxes one of the least of these commandments and teaches others to do the same will be called least in the kingdom of heaven, but whoever does them and teaches them will be called great in the kingdom of heaven. For I tell you, unless your righteousness exceeds that of the scribes and Pharisees, you will never enter the kingdom of heaven. (Matt. 5:17-20)

Jesus' position toward the law is discussed in more detail in my book *The Mystery of the Historical Jesus: The Messiah in the Qur'an, the Bible, and Historical Sources* (pp. 377-388).

God assigned another specific task to Jesus. He charged him with delivering the good news about the coming of a future prophet:

> When Jesus son of Mary said: "O Children of Israel! I am a messenger of Allah to you, confirming that which was revealed before me of the Torah, and bringing good news about a messenger who will come after me, whose name is Aḥmad." But when he came to them with clear proofs, they said: "This is clear magic." (61.6)

The name of the promised Prophet, "Aḥmad," shares the root *ḥamd* (praise) with "Muḥammad." Muḥammad means "highly praised" or "highly celebrated." Aḥmad is a comparative which some suggest means "more praised" and others "more praising." This Prophet was mentioned in both the Torah of Moses and the Injīl of Jesus:

> Those (the believers) who follow the Messenger, the unlettered Prophet, whom they find mentioned in the Torah and the Injīl which they have: He will enjoin on them that which is right and forbid them that which is evil; he will make lawful for them all good things and prohibit for them only the foul; and he will relieve them of their burden and the yokes that are upon them. Those who believe in him, honor him, help him, and follow the light that is sent down with him — those are the successful. (7.157)

As Jesus lived about 6 centuries before Prophet Muhammad (570-

632 CE), his foretelling of the coming of Muhammad and confirmation of his prophethood were particularly important for two main reasons. **First**, by the time Prophet Muhammad appeared, there were millions of Christians in various countries, including a small minority in Arabia. Jesus had to tell those Christians to accept the new prophet whose message continued his original teachings. By the time of Muhammad's appearance, Christianity had become fundamentally different form the religion that Jesus taught, so the coming of the new prophet gave Christians an opportunity to drop those false doctrines and follow Jesus' authentic teachings that the preaching of the new Prophet reflected. But only some Christians followed the new prophet, as most did not. Obeying Jesus' command by most or many of his followers would have resulted in a very different history from the one we know today — the history that should have been, rather than the history that is.

Second, the Qur'an tells us that every prophet testified to the verity of the prophets who preceded him and confirmed their messages. For instance, Muhammad confirmed the messages of Jesus, Moses, Aaron, and the other prophets who came before him; Jesus confirmed the messages of Moses, Aaron, and the earlier prophets; and so on. However, Muhammad was destined to be the last of God's prophets:

> Muhammad is not the father of any of your men, but he is the Messenger of Allah and the Last of the prophets; and Allah has full knowledge of all things. (33.40)

Muhammad's prophethood was not going to be confirmed by a later prophet, so it was confirmed *in advance* by the prophet who came before him, Jesus, as well as by other earlier prophets.

The description of Jesus' mission in the Qur'an is very different from how many modern scholars of the historical Jesus see it. They fundamentally view him as a "Jew," even though they may have differences about what he said and did. What they mean by that is that Jesus grew up among the Jews, believed in what they believed in, and did what he tried to do while acting as a Jew. This image, however, reflects a misunderstanding of what the term "Jew" means.

The Biblical term "Jew" came to denote all adherents of Judaism, the Qur'an gives a completely different meaning for the term. The Qur'an implies that this term did not exist before Moses or, more accurately, the Torah. In other words, it was coined by God Himself, as He coined the term "Muslim" (22.78). It is a name for those who believed in Moses' message and embraced his religion, regardless of their ethnic origin. Naturally, it is not a name that applies to their leader, Moses. Similarly, the name of Jesus' followers in the Qur'an, *Naṣārā*, is not applied to Jesus.

Calling Jesus a "Jew" is the result of misunderstanding what this term originally meant. But it also reflects the attempt by scholars to minimize the scale of Jesus' mission and role. I think the attempt to present Jesus as no more than a Jew is partly influenced by the fact that he did not become a major character in Jewish Palestine at the time. He managed to get only a very small minority of Jews to accept that he was a legitimate successor of Moses who came to reform his message that has long been corrupted by various religious authorities. But this very limited success should not distract from what he tried to do. Jesus' role as a "prophet" in the Qur'an makes him a major spiritual leader like Moses and Muhammad, even though his message was more local.

The attempt to present Jesus as a Jew is probably also partly influenced by the attempt of modern scholars to bring Christians and Jews closer and further expose the unwarranted nature of the hostility and prosecution that Christians subjected the Jews to for centuries. As one scholar has noted, "Conceiving of Jesus as a 'Jew' in the modern era and especially since the Second World War and the Holocaust, has had the merit of locating him, his family, his initial followers, and his world of vision and memory properly within the House of Israel, rather than imagining them, as did German National Socialist exegetes and anti-Semites, as some kind of 'Aryans' or non-Semites" (Elliot, 2007: 151).

Some scholars have argued that Jesus should be called "Israelite" not "Jew." They argue that the latter is a late misnomer that did not exist in Jesus' days. The Jews used to refer to themselves as "Israelites" or "Hebrews" and other people used to call them a term that is better translated as "Judeans" rather than "Jews," as it is derived from Judea, where the Israelites lived after coming back from exile in Babylon (Elliot, 2007). But these scholars share with others their keenness on not differentiating Jesus from other people as they see his mission much smaller than it was as they measure its scope in terms of its very limited success rather than in terms of what it really aimed to achieve.

For more details about the origin and etymology of the term "Jew" in the Bible and the Qur'an, the reader may consult our book *The Mystery of Israel in Ancient Egypt* (2008b, 184-187).

The Messiah would never scorn to be a servant to Allah, nor would the angels who are nearest to Allah. As for those who scorn His service and are arrogantly proud, He shall gather them all to Himself to answer.

(Qur'an, 4.172)

2

The Human Historical Messiah

The concept of "Messiah" is found in Judaism, Christianity, and Islam. Islam confirms Christianity's claim that Jesus was the Messiah, so it disagrees with Judaism which rejects Jesus and teaches that the Messiah is yet to come. But when it comes to its view on the nature of the Messiah, Islam's position with respect to the other two Abrahamic religions reverses. Islam agrees with Judaism that the Messiah was a human being not a god, so it rejects the Christian deification of Jesus.

In this chapter, I will give a comparative overview of the concept of "Messiah" in the three great religions.

The Human Jewish Messiah

The Hebrew term *Mashiaḥ* means the "anointed one." It's origin is the practice of pouring oil on an object, to mark its dedication to God, or on the head of a person, to denote God's support of the anointed person for a particular mission or position of leadership.

The Old Testament uses the term "Messiah" 39 times, applying it to a number of different individuals who held various positions. Kings (1 Sam. 10:1, 1 Sam. 16:12-13), priests (Exo. 40:12-15), and prophets (Isa. 61:1; 1 Kings 19:15-16) were anointed. The people of Israel are also called "Messiah" (1 Chr. 16:15-22; Ps. 105:8-15). This title is applied in the Old Testament even to a non-Israelite, King Cyrus of Persia. After defeating the Babylonians, Cyrus allowed the Jews, who had been taken from Jerusalem into exile in Babylon by the Babylonian king Nebuchadnezzar II, to return to their homeland.

All of these historical "anointed" individuals were human beings. The Old Testament does not suggest any of them had any divine quality, so the term "Messiah" is not associated with any form of divinity.

The Old Testament also contains a number of prophecies about future figures who would come to defeat Israel's enemy and re-establish the lost kingdom of the chosen nation of God. Unlike the historical Messiahs discussed earlier, none of these future salvational figures of Israel was given the title "Messiah" in the Old Testament. These scriptural passages started to be spoken of as "messianic" prophecies or expectations only after the saviors they talk about started all to be seen as representing *one anointed* eschatological figure whose coming would usher a new world order.

Like the historical figures called Messiahs, none of these military future saviors was given any divine attributes. The human nature of these kings is implied in the fact that they were all descendants of David.

Other Jewish sources portray different Messiahs. For instance, the Dead Sea Scrolls, which date from the 2nd century BCE to the 1st century CE, talk about two awaited Messiahs. In addition to the one who descended from David the king, the other Messiah is a descendant of Aaron, Moses' brother, the priest. Again, both Messiahs are clearly descendants of human beings.

So Jewish sources do not attribute to anyone that it calls "Messiah" or associates with messianic expectations any form of divinity. This is natural because Judaism believes in one God only.

The Divine Christ

Judaism and Christianity accept the verity of the concept of the "Messiah," and Christianity has inherited a number of the attributes that Judaism conferred on the Messiah. But contrary to what Christians believe, Judaism did not see the Messiah as a central figure, whereas Christianity is founded on and around the "Christ," the Greek word for "Messiah."

One fundamental difference between the two religions is that Judaism does not recognize Jesus as the Messiah. The reason is that Jesus' life did not fit the Jewish profile of the awaited Messiah. For instance, he did not come as a nationalist leader and warrior whose goal is to restore Israel's lost glory. Jesus led a completely peaceful life and avoided any conflict with the political establishment. He stressed that he was a spiritual not military figure and resisted any attempt by people to get him involved in a conflict with the Roman political leadership. This was a major factor in the rejection of most Jews of Jesus' claim to messiahship (Fatoohi, 2009: 39-40).

The Jews had to choose between accepting Jesus' correction of the concept of the Messiah and adhering to their centuries-old distorted portrait of the Messiah, and they chose tradition to correction. The

Christians, on the other hand, choose to redefine those traditional attributes to make them applicable to Jesus.

Also, the Christ was killed on the cross, whereas the Jewish Messiah was going to be victorious and successfully restore the kingdom of Israel. The concept of a suffering Messiah has no Jewish origin (Fatoohi, 2009: 75-77).

Another difference between Jesus and the Jewish Messiah is that the latter was a human being, whereas Christianity gave its Messiah divine attributes. A divine Messiah is not a Jewish concept but a Christian invention. It had no roots in history before Paul, the writer of the Gospel of John, and other early theologians developed Christianity to what it came to be. It is an irony that Christianity claims to accept Judaism as a revealed religion and the Old Testament as divine scripture yet it has designed a Messiah that is fundamentally different from the Jewish one.

The Human *Masīh* of the Qur'an

Unlike the Old Testament, the Qur'an talks about one Messiah, and it identifies this Messiah as Jesus. Jesus is called *al-Masīh* (the Messiah) 11 times in 9 different Qur'anic verses.

The Qur'anic Messiah shares very little similarity with the Christian Messiah and even less with the Jewish one. Apart from identifying the Messiah with Jesus and presenting him as a miracle worker, the Qur'anic Messiah shares none of the attributes of the Christian Messiah.

The Qur'anic Messiah was not a royal and he did not descend from King David. Having been born of virginal conception, so he did not have a father, he is only called after his mother, "son of Mary."

Jesus was not a warrior or a military leader. He had no political agenda and led a peaceful life. He had a spiritual mission like that of any prophet.

The Jewish Messiah is an eschatological figure who would come just before the end of times. Jesus' followers had to modify this concept, because he left without triggering the end of the world, so they invented the concept of Jesus' second coming and placed it at the end of times. The Qur'an does not present the Messiah as an eschatological figure. He lived, died, and will be resurrected on the Day of Resurrection like everyone else. The Qur'an rejects presenting Jesus as a unique kind of prophet and it refutes portraying the

Messiah's appearance as the climax of history. Jesus was very much part of history in the same way that every other prophet was.

One attribute that the Qur'anic Jesus shares with the Jewish Messiah is his human nature. As explained earlier, Jesus was a Muslim prophet and messenger — a servant of God.

For more information about the concept of "Messiah" in Judaism, Christianity, and Islam, the reader may like to consult my book *The Mystery of the Messiah: Jesus' Messiahship in the Qur'an, the New Testament, the Old Testament, and other Jewish.*

Part II

"Son of Mary" Not "Son of God"

3. The Non-Divine Jewish "Sonship of God" 35
4. The Christian "Sonship of God" 39
   Christian Sons of God 39
   The Unique Son of God 41
   The Eternal Son of John 45
   When Did Jesus' Sonship of God become Special? 48
   Sonship of God, Messiahship, and Miracle Working 52
   Sonship of God and Blasphemy 53
5. The Qur'an's Rejection of the "Sonship of God" 57
   The Oneness of God 57
   No Offspring of God 59
   Jesus' False "Sonship of God" 63
6. Son of Man 73
   The Unhistorical Link Between "Son of Man" and "Messiah" 73
   Jesus' Use of the Term "Son of Man" 78

And the Jews and the Christians say: "We are the sons of Allah and His beloved ones." Say [O Muhammad!]: "Why does He then chastise you for your faults? No, you are human beings from among those whom He has created; He forgives whom He pleases and chastises whom He pleases."

(Qur'an, 5.18)

3

The Non-Divine Jewish "Sonship of God"

Only the title "Christ" rivals the popularity of Jesus' epithet "son of God." Christianity did not invent the concept of "sonship of God" but inherited it from Judaism. However, Christianity changed this concept fundamentally by extending its meaning to imply divine qualities — something it never had in Judaism.

The title "son of God" is used in the Old Testament in four distinct ways:

(1) It is used for unidentified non-human beings:

> When man began to multiply on the face of the land and daughters were born to them, the *sons of God* saw that the daughters of man were attractive. And they took as their wives any they chose. Then the Lord said, "My Spirit shall not abide in man forever, for he is flesh: his days shall be 120 years." The Nephilim were on the earth in those days, and also afterward, when the *sons of God* came in to the daughters of man and they bore children to them. These were the mighty men who were of old, the men of renown. (Gen. 6:1-4)

The same Hebrew expression, *beney ha'elohim*, is found again only in the Book of Job where it is used for angels, suggesting that they are the unidentified non-human creatures of Genesis (also Job 2:1, 38:7):

> Now there was a day when the *sons of God* came to present themselves before the Lord, and Satan also came among them. (Job 1:6)

A very similar Hebrew expression with the same meaning, *beney 'elim*, in the Book of Psalms (29:1, 89:6) also denotes angelic beings.

(2) King David is described as the "son of God" and God is called his father. Speaking to the Prophet Nathan, God said about David: "I will be to him a father, and he shall be to me a son" (2 Sam. 7:14). In one of the Psalms, the king says: "I will tell of the decree: The Lord said to me, 'You are my Son; today I have begotten you'" (Ps. 2:7).

(3) All of Israel is described as God's son (Hos. 11:1). This is part of God's instructions to Moses:

Then you shall say to Pharaoh, "Thus says the Lord, Israel is my firstborn son, and I say to you, 'Let my son go that he may serve me.' If you refuse to let him go, behold, I will kill your firstborn son." (Exo. 4:22-23)

(4) In post-Biblical periods the title "son of God" started to be applied only to pious Jews, as in the following passage from the apocryphal Book of Jubilees, which is dated to the middle of the 2nd century BCE:

And the Lord said to Moses: "I know their contrariness and their thoughts and their stiffneckedness, and they will not be obedient till they confess their own sin and the sin of their fathers. And after this they will turn to Me in all uprightness and with all (their) heart and with all (their) soul, and I will circumcise the foreskin of their heart and the foreskin of the heart of their seed, and I will create in them a holy spirit, and I will cleanse them so that they shall not turn away from Me from that day unto eternity. And their souls will cleave to Me and to all My commandments, and they will fulfill My commandments, and I will be their Father and they shall be My children. And they all shall be called children of the living God, and every angel and every spirit shall know, yes, they shall know that these are My children, and that I am their Father in uprightness and righteousness, and that I love them." (Jub. 1:21-24)

According to the 1st century BCE Book of the Psalms of Solomon, the Messiah will purify the Jews, who will then become "sons of their God":

And he shall gather together a holy people, whom he shall lead in righteousness,
And he shall judge the tribes of the people that has been sanctified by the Lord his God.
And he shall not suffer unrighteousness to lodge any more in their midst,
Nor shall there dwell with them any man that knows wickedness,
For he shall know them, that they are all sons of their God.
And he shall divide them according to their tribes upon the land,
And neither sojourner nor alien shall sojourn with them anymore. (PsSol. 17)

Vermes (2000: 32) suggests that in the 2nd century BCE, the title "son of God" started to be applied to the awaited royal Messiah, but other scholars contend that this was never a title of the Messiah (Miller, 2003: 224).

In all four Jewish uses, the title "son of God" is always used as a figure of speech. A son of God is someone who is close to God, but he does not share the divinity of God. Sonship of God does not mean that the person is divine, even when applied to individuals who are deemed to be particularly close to God. The Talmud states that two renowned Jewish miracle workers were called *sons of God*. One of these was Honi who lived around the middle of the 1st century BCE and developed fame for successfully praying for rain by drawing a magical circle. In one prayer, in which he calls himself a *member of God's house*, Honi calls the Jews *God's children*:

> Master of the Universe, *Thy children* have turned to me because [they believe] me to be a *member of Thy house*. I swear by Thy great name that I will not move from here until you have mercy upon *Thy children*! (Ta'an. 23a)

The second miracle worker is the healer Hanina ben Dosa who lived in the 1st century CE, about one generation after Jesus. Hanina is reported to have performed many miracles, some similar to Jesus'. One Talmudic account claims that a divine voice used to call Hanina "My son" (Bera. 17b):

> Rab Judah said in the name of Rab: Every day a Heavenly Voice is heard declaring, the whole world draws its sustenance because [of the merit] of Hanina *my son*, and Hanina *my son* suffices himself with a kab of carobs from one Sabbath eve to another. (Ta'an. 24b)

This sonship of God did not mean to the Rabbi writers of the Talmud or to its Jewish readers that Honi or Hanina had any divine attributes or were more than human beings. They were merely considered to be close to God and that nearness is seen as the cause of their abilities to perform miracles. This nearness to God is different from the concept sonship of God in Roman polytheistic religions where it denoted divinity. Judaism restricted divinity to God. This is the main difference between the Jewish use of the title "son of God" and its use in Christianity. So while it is true that Christianity did not invent the concept of sonship of God but inherited it from Judaism, it developed it to something completely different from its Jewish origin.

Surely they disbelieve those who say: "Allah is the Messiah son of Mary." The Messiah himself said: "O Children of Israel! Worship Allah, my Lord and your Lord. Whoever joins other gods with Allah, for him Allah has forbidden paradise. His abode is the Fire. The evildoers shall have no helpers."

(Qur'an, 5.72)

4

The Christian "Sonship of God"

The title "son of God" is applied to Jesus not only in the canon, but in apocryphal sources also. For instance, in the Arabic Gospel of the Infancy idols are made to tell Egyptian priests that Jesus was the *son of God* (AraIn. 4:11). Studying the use of this term in apocryphal writings, however, adds almost nothing to what we can already learn from the New Testament, so we will focus on the latter.

Jesus is called the "son of God" numerous times in the New Testament, but the authors used this term in a number of different ways and gave it various connotations and meanings. Before we study the different usages, we need to be aware of evidence that suggests that this significant title was at times added by the Evangelists. More specifically, the title "son of God" appears in Matthew's version of some events but is absent from Mark's account of the same events (e.g. Mark 6:47-51; Matt. 14:24-33). In one example Mark (8:29) makes Peter say that people thought that Jesus was "the Christ" but in Matthew's (16:16) account Peter's words have an interesting addition: "the Christ, the Son of the living God." Given that it is generally accepted that Mark's Gospel is older than Matthew's and Luke's and that these two were partly based on the former, we should conclude that in such instances Matthew has discretionally added the title "Son of God" to the original text.

Comparing texts of the same event in different Gospels can reveal such significant changes and additions. But, unfortunately, straightforward comparisons are not always possible, and it is often difficult to identify changes to the text. This caveat should be kept in mind as we look into the different meanings of the title "son of God" in the Gospels, although this warning applies to the study of the New Testament in general.

Christian Sons of God

The term "son of God" was not applied to Jesus only in the New Testament. Jesus himself used the phrase "your father" in reference to

God around 20 times in his sermons. In the majority of these instances (e.g. Mark 11:25; Luke 6:35; John 20:17), he was addressing his disciples, i.e. he called them *sons of God*:

> Let your light shine before others, so that they may see your good works and give glory to *your Father* who is in heaven. (Matt. 5:16)
>
> Fear not, little flock, for it is *your Father's* good pleasure to give you the kingdom. (Luke 12:32)

In one instance (Matt. 5:9), Jesus described "peacemakers" as "sons of God."

In a confused account in John in which Jesus argues with people who are described as "had believed in him" (John 8:31) and who call God *their father* (John 8:41), Jesus accuses them of not accepting his teachings and goes on to label them as *sons of the devil* (John 8:42-44). This suggests that Jesus called God the father of the believers only. It also shows that the terms *son of God*, like *son of devil*, is used figuratively. The following passage, in which Jesus addresses his disciples, seems to suggest that only those who do good works would be sons of God:

> But love your enemies, and do good, and lend, expecting nothing in return, and your reward will be great, and you will be sons of the Most High, for he is kind to the ungrateful and the evil. Be merciful, even as your Father is merciful. (Luke 6:35-36)

First John also contains passages that seem to restrict the sonship of God to the righteous (also 1 John 5:1, 5:18):

> If you know that he is righteous, you may be sure that everyone who practices righteousness has been *born of him*. (1 John 2:29)
>
> No one *born of God* makes a practice of sinning, for God's seed abides in him, and he cannot keep on sinning because he has been *born of God*. (1 John 3:9)

This restrictive use of the term is similar to its exclusive application in post-Biblical times to pious Jews (p. 36).

Paul applies the term *sons of God* to *all Israelites*: "They are Israelites, and to them belong the *adoption*, the glory, the covenants, the giving of the law, the worship, and the promises" (Rom. 9:4). Luke (3:38) calls Adam also the son of God.

Jesus' reported application of the sonship of God to the righteous and not only himself and its application by New Testament writers to people are in line with the historical fact that this concept did not imply divinity and, therefore, was never considered blasphemous. As we shall see later in this chapter, the Jewish leaders' alleged accusation of Jesus of blasphemy for claiming to be the son of God is unhistorical. The four Evangelists attributed to the Jewish accusers of Jesus their own, late understanding of the concept of *sonship of God*. The Jews of the time of Jesus, like those who lived before him, never understood the term in this way.

The *Unique* Son of God

While the Evangelists and other New Testament writers state that Jesus and others described various people as sons of God, the following peculiar Johannine passages state that the title "son of God" was actually Jesus' only:

> For God so loved the world, that he gave his *only* Son, that whoever believes in him should not perish but have eternal life. (John 3:16)
>
> Whoever believes in him is not condemned, but whoever does not believe is condemned already, because he has not believed in the name of the *only* Son of God. (John 3:18)
>
> In this the love of God was made manifest among us, that God sent his *only* Son into the world, so that we might live through him. (1 John 4:9)

Reconciling these with passages in which the title "son of God" is applied to others would require the assumption that Jesus was considered as a *special and unique son of God*. While believers are sons of God, Jesus is *The Son of God* and the "only son" (John 1:14, 3:16). This could then explain the title "the Son," which appears once in each of the Synoptics (Mark 13:32; Matt. 11:27; Luke 10:22) and a number of times in the Gospel of John and First John. Jesus is also called God's "beloved son" (Mark 1:11, 9:7; Matt. 3:17, 17:5; Luke 3:22) and the *chosen son* (Luke 9:35).

It may be assumed that this specific sense of "son of God" is what the Jewish leaders objected to and led them to accuse Jesus of blasphemy and ask for his death. This would solve the historical problem in this account, which I highlighted earlier. But this assumption has no supportive evidence. The Jewish leaders are shown as being angry at the very claim to sonship of God.

In the following passage, John states that Jesus' claim to the sonship of God was considered blasphemous because it was understood to have made him equal to God:

And this was why the Jews were persecuting Jesus, because he was doing these things on the Sabbath. But Jesus answered them, "*My Father is working until now, and I am working.*" This was why the Jews were seeking all the more to kill him, because not only was he breaking the Sabbath, but he was even *calling God his own Father, making himself equal with God.* (John 5:16-18)

There is actually nothing in what Jesus said and did here that would justify the Jewish leaders' conclusion that he was claiming equality with God. It looks like John believed that this equality with the Divine is what enraged the law experts and made them charge Jesus with blasphemy so he decided to introduce it here even though the context did not justify it.

However, among the over 40 Gospel passages in which Jesus uses the term "my father" and others in which he talks about "the father" there are some that reflect a special intimacy and unique relationship between the son and his father. The question is then whether some of them express the uniqueness of Jesus' sonship of God in terms that could be interpreted as blasphemous.

Confirming Jesus' special sonship of God, the author of Hebrews asks polemically: "To which of the angels did God ever say, 'You are my Son, today I have begotten you'? Or again, 'I will be to him a father, and he shall be to me a son'?" (Heb. 1:5).

The writer of First John links the son of God to eternal life, as it is through the belief in the son of God eternal life is earned: "God gave us eternal life, and this life is in his Son. Whoever has the Son has life; whoever does not have the Son of God does not have life. I write these things to you who believe in the name of the Son of God that you may know that you have eternal life" (1 John 5:11-13). In the following two passages, the Evangelists state that the father gave his son Jesus the special authority to acknowledge or deny people before God, and made him the only way to the father:

> So everyone who acknowledges me before men, I also will acknowledge before my Father who is in heaven, but whoever denies me before men, I also will deny before my Father who is in heaven. (Matt. 10:32-33)

> Jesus said to him, "I am the way, and the truth, and the life. No one comes to the Father except through me." (John 14:6)

This unique son has been handed everything that the father has: "All that the Father has is mine" (John 16:15). He is a mystery that no one knows other than his father (also Luke 10:22):

> All things have been handed over to me by my Father, and no one knows the Son except the Father, and no one knows the Father except the Son and anyone to whom the Son chooses to reveal him. (Matt. 11:27)

It is the Evangelist John who stresses in the most striking way the uniqueness of Jesus' sonship of God, stretching its meaning far beyond what the other Evangelists ever thought, making it confer on Jesus the God-like status that became accepted by most Christians. John's descriptions of this special son of God blur the differences between him and his father. Among what the father has handed to his unique son, according to John, is the ability to lay down his life and take it back:

> For this reason the Father loves me, because I lay down my life that I may take it up again. No one takes it from me, but I lay it down of my own accord. I have authority to lay it down, and I have authority to take it up again. This charge I have received from my Father. (John 10:17-18)

God has even given his special son the authority to raise people from the dead on the Day of Resurrection:

> For this is the will of my Father, that everyone who looks on the Son and believes in him should have eternal life, and I will raise him up on the last day. (John 6:40)

This ability to raise the dead is stressed in another Johannine passage which goes even further as it lists the powers that this son has from his father:

> For as the Father raises the dead and gives them life, so also the Son gives life to whom he will. The Father judges no one, but has given all judgment to the Son, that all may honor the Son, just as they honor the Father. Whoever does not honor the Son does not honor the Father who sent him. Truly, truly, I say to you, whoever hears my word and believes him who sent me has eternal life. He does not come into judgment, but has passed from death to life. "Truly, truly, I say to you, an hour is coming, and is now here, when the dead will hear the voice of the Son of God, and those who hear will live. For as the Father has life in himself, so he has granted the Son also to have life in himself. And he has given him authority to execute judgment, because he is the Son of Man. Do not marvel at this, for an hour is coming when all who are in the tombs will hear his voice and come out, those who have done good to the resurrection of life, and those who have done evil to the resurrection of judgment. "I can do nothing on my own. As I hear, I judge, and my

judgment is just, because I seek not my own will but the will of him who sent me." (John 5:21-30)

Like many other New Testament passages, this pericope promotes the father and the son as two distinct beings, but it does that in a strange way, as the more John tells us about the specialness and uniqueness of this son the less clear the difference between him and his father becomes. This Evangelist makes his Jesus say that seeing him is seeing the father, and that he is in the father and the father is in him (John 10:38):

> If you had known me, you would have known my Father also. From now on you do know him and have seen him. Philip said to him, "Lord, show us the Father, and it is enough for us." Jesus said to him, "Have I been with you so long, and you still do not know me, Philip? *Whoever has seen me has seen the Father.* How can you say, 'Show us the Father'? Do you not believe that *I am in the Father and the Father is in me*? The words that I say to you I do not speak on my own authority, but *the Father who dwells in me* does his works. Believe me that *I am in the Father and the Father is in me*, or else believe on account of the works themselves." (John 14:7-11)

Any meaningful distinction between the son and the father is explicitly denied when John makes Jesus tell Jewish leaders: "I and the Father are one" (John 10:30)! This relationship of oneness is encountered again in Jesus' prayer to the father:

> And I am no longer in the world, but they are in the world, and I am coming to you. Holy Father, keep them in your name, which you have given me, that they may be one, even as *we are one*. (John 17:11)

John goes on to spell out what this unity between the son and the father exactly means in an equally stark fashion in a dialog between the resurrected Jesus and Thomas in which the disciple declares unequivocally that Jesus is God:

> Then he said to Thomas, "Put your finger here, and see my hands; and put out your hand, and place it in my side. Do not disbelieve, but believe." Thomas answered him, "My Lord and *my God*!" (John 20:27-28)

In summary, while the Synoptists described Jesus as a special and unique son of God, John took this concept well beyond what the other Evangelists thought. He gave the concept of "son of God," albeit a *special* sonship, dimensions that it never knew in the history of the monotheistic Judaism.

Paul, the earliest of the New Testament authors, also believed that Jesus was divine. Talking about the Israelites, he goes on to say: "From their race, according to the flesh, is the *Christ who is God over all*" (Rom. 9:5). This descent of the Divine as a human being is what Paul means when he describes Jesus as having been "descended from David according to the flesh" (Rom. 1:3). Unlike Adam who was "from the earth," Paul's Jesus came "from heaven" (1 Cor. 15:47). He states that Jesus was "in the form of God" (Phi. 2:6).

Other New Testament authors have also declared the divinity of Jesus. For instance, the Book of Titus, which most scholars do not think was written by Paul despite attributing itself to the apostle, talks of "our great God and Savior Jesus Christ" (Tit. 2:13).

The *Eternal* Son of John

The way in which John reconciled talking about Jesus and God as two distinct beings with making them also one and the same further underlines the fundamental difference between his theology and the theologies of the Synoptists. John claimed that although Jesus was born and sent at some point in time, which is how he is distinct from the eternal father, he was actually an embodiment of the Word, which existed from eternity. He starts his Gospel as follows:

> In the beginning was the Word, and the Word was with God, and the Word was God. He was in the beginning with God. (John 1:1-2)

He later tells us that this Word took the form of a human being, Jesus, and came to live with people on earth:

> And the Word became flesh and dwelt among us, and we have seen his glory, glory as of the only Son from the Father, full of grace and truth. (John 1:14)

One passage quotes Jesus praying: "Father, glorify me in your own presence with the glory that I had with you *before the world existed*" (John 17:5). Jesus' preexistence and coexistence with God is again confirmed in that prayer as Jesus goes on to say: "You loved me *before the foundation of the world*" (John 17:24). Jesus is also quoted as telling a Jewish audience that he existed before Abraham — a claim that triggered an attempt by the angry listeners to stone him in response to what they perceived as some form of blasphemy (John 8:58-59).

The Evangelist also has John the Baptist declare that Jesus existed before him, implying again that Jesus' existence predated his physical appearance in this world:

> John bore witness about him, and cried out, "This was he of whom I said, 'He who comes after me ranks before me, because *he was before me*'" (John 1:15)

The Book of Colossians, which many reject its attribution to Paul, shares John's claims, calling Jesus "the firstborn of all creation" (Col. 1:15). It then goes on to more emphatically stress Jesus' preexistence saying that "all things were created through him and for him" (Col. 1:16). The author of Hebrews also calls Jesus "the firstborn" and further claims that the angels were ordered to worship him: "When he brings the firstborn into the world, he says, 'Let all God's angels worship him.'" There is significant similarity between this passage and the Qur'anic account of God's asking the angels to prostrate for Adam (also 7.11, 18.50, 20.116):

> And when We said to the angels: "Prostrate yourselves before Adam," so they fell prostrate except Iblīs. He refused and waxed proud, so he became one of the disbelievers. (2.34)

> And when We said to the angels: "Prostrate yourselves before Adam," so they fell prostrate except Iblīs. He said: "Shall I fall prostrate before one whom you have created of clay?" (17.61)

This looks to be another instance of "contextual displacement." In the Qur'anic account, Adam is the *firstborn* of his kind and the angels were commanded to pay homage to him as the representative of a new species that was destined to produce spiritually highly developed individuals, such as the prophets. Satan felt that the fact that he was created of fire, as he was a jinn, gave him a higher status than an individual made originally of clay, so he rejected God's command. God threw him out of the special place in which he was living and became the Devil who wants to make the human beings reject and disobey God to prove his point and exact revenge. It looks like this original account was changed and reproduced by some Christian theologians, including the author of Hebrews, to make Jesus the firstborn, which made him eternal, and make the angel *worship* him, which made him divine.

John also described Jesus as primordial light:

> The true light, which enlightens everyone, was coming into the world. He was in the world, and the world was made through him, yet the world

did not know him. He came to his own, and his own people did not receive him. (John 1:9-11)

John stresses a number of times in his Gospel that Jesus came from God and returned to Him:

Now before the Feast of the Passover, when Jesus knew that his hour had come to depart out of this world to the Father, having loved his own who were in the world, he loved them to the end. During supper, when the devil had already put it into the heart of Judas Iscariot, Simon's son, to betray him, Jesus, knowing that the Father had given all things into his hands, and that he had come from God and was going back to God. (John 13:1-3)

For the Father himself loves you, because you have loved me and have believed that I came from God. I came from the Father and have come into the world, and now I am leaving the world and going to the Father. (John 16:27-28)

John's Jesus was with God from eternity, became flesh and came to live with people, and then left them and went back to where he originally came from: God. John's Jesus is clearly divine. John obviously promotes the doctrine of the Incarnation.

John still has passages that portray Jesus as having a lower status than the father. For instance, Jesus proclaims that he was sent by the father (John 20:21), the father is greater than him (John 14:28), and he is under the command of the father (John 12:49, 14:31). There is clear inconsistency in John's portrayal of the divine Jesus and his relationship with God. As has been rightly pointed out, with his "plain affirmation of the pre-eminence of the Father contradicting all the metaphors which suggest equality, John created a doctrinal problem the resolution of which kept the church, the councils, the bishops, and the theologians fully occupied for several centuries" (Vermes, 2000: 48).

John's doctrine of the Word, or *Logos* in Greek, is believed to have been inspired by the Alexandrian Jewish philosopher Philo (ca. 15 BCE – ca. 45 CE) who taught that the Logos was the intermediary between God and the cosmos, as it is God's tool of creation and the agent through which the human mind can apprehend and comprehend God. The idea of the Logos dates back to the 6th century BC Greek philosopher Heraclitus who believed that the cosmic processes have a logos, or reason, similar to the reasoning power in man. The concept was developed further by other Greek philosophers. Vermes suggests that John's Logos doctrine was also influenced by

Hermetism. According to this 1st century CE pagan Hellenistic mysticism, deification of man is achieved through knowledge, and the Logos is referred to as the "son of God" (Vermes, 2000: 51).

I should point out that the Qur'anic concept of the divine word *kun* (be) is completely different from the concept of the Logos. This is one verse in which this concept is used:

> [He is] the Originator of the heavens and the earth! When He decrees a matter, He says to it "*Be!*" and it is (2.117).

This concept is not something that can take a form of or be represented by a being, and it has nothing to do with man's ability or, more accurately, the lack of it to comprehend God. Philo's idea that the Logos is God's agent of creation may seem closer to the Qur'anic concept of *kun* (be), but that is not the case. The latter is merely a symbolic expression of God's limitless power and His ability to do whatever He wants whenever He likes. We have discussed elsewhere in more detail the Qur'anic concept of *kun* (Fatoohi, 2007: 96-97).

When Did Jesus' Sonship of God become Special?

For John, Jesus existed and was divine from eternity, which is what made him a special son of God. The author of Hebrews (1:2) states that God created the world through Jesus, which also implies that Jesus is eternal. But Paul and the Synoptists favored different versions of an alternative doctrine that came to be known as "adoptionism." This doctrine was widespread in the first three centuries of Christianity before its opponents succeeded in suppressing it and turned it into a heresy. It states that Jesus was adopted at some point by God as his special son.

Naturally, Christian theologians who believe that Jesus was always divine reject adoptionism. One argument they make is that there is no passage in the New Testament suggesting that Jesus *became* at some point God's son (e.g. Witmer, 1998: 50). The fact is that there are passages each of which can only mean that Jesus became God's son, i.e. his special son, at a specific point. It is also true that Paul and the Synoptists do not say that Jesus was eternal. Furthermore, they make statements that clearly disagree with the view that John promoted.

Although Paul believed that Jesus was a human incarnation of God, he also believed that Jesus became *the* son of God by virtue of his resurrection:

Concerning his Son, who was descended from David according to the flesh and was declared to be the Son of God in power according to the Spirit of holiness *by his resurrection from the dead*, Jesus Christ our Lord. (Rom. 1:3-4)

Have this mind among yourselves, which is yours in Christ Jesus, who, though he was in the form of God, did not count equality with God a thing to be grasped, but made himself nothing, taking the form of a servant, being born in the likeness of men. And being found in human form, he humbled himself by becoming obedient to the point of death, even death on a cross. Therefore God has highly exalted him and bestowed on him the name that is above every name, so that at the name of Jesus every knee should bow, in heaven and on earth and under the earth, and every tongue confess that Jesus Christ is Lord, to the glory of God the Father. (Phi. 2:5-11)

In another passage that Acts attributes to Paul, the apostle is quoted as saying: "And we bring you the good news that what God promised to the fathers, this he has fulfilled to us their children *by raising Jesus*, as also it is written in the second Psalm, 'You are my Son, *today I have begotten you*'" (Acts 13:32-33). Here also God's special fatherhood of Jesus is said to have happened after he was raised. Paul is quoting from the Book of Psalms in which David says that when God made him king He told him: "You are my Son; today I have begotten you" (Ps. 2:7).

Paul's passages above talk about Jesus being a son of God but not necessarily a *unique* or *only* son. But since Paul believed that Jesus was already a human incarnation of God (Rom. 9:5, 1:3; 1 Cor. 15.47), he must have meant that the crucifixion and resurrection made Jesus a *special* son of God.

Mark, whose Gospel was written at least two decades after Paul's letters, identifies a different transformation point that made Jesus the special son of God: his baptism. After being baptized by John and as he was coming out of the water, Jesus saw "the heavens being torn open and the Spirit descending on him like a dove." He then heard a voice from heaven say: "*You are my beloved Son*; with you I am well pleased" (Mark 1:10-11).

As Mark's Gospel starts with Jesus' encounter with John, there is no earlier event that signifies Jesus' special status as God's only son.

Mark mentions another event in which Jesus' special status as *the* son of God is stressed, which is Jesus' transfiguration:

And after six days Jesus took with him Peter and James and John, and led them up a high mountain by themselves. And he was transfigured before them, and his clothes became radiant, intensely white, as no one on earth could bleach them. And there appeared to them Elijah with Moses, and they were talking with Jesus. And Peter said to Jesus, "Rabbi, it is good that we are here. Let us make three tents, one for you and one for Moses and one for Elijah." For he did not know what to say, for they were terrified. And a cloud overshadowed them, and a voice came out of the cloud, "*This is my beloved Son*; listen to him." And suddenly, looking around, they no longer saw anyone with them but Jesus only. (Mark 9:2-8)

It is speculative to suggest that the transfiguration represents another level of exaltation of Jesus' status, because the voice from the cloud did not add anything new to the words of the heavenly voice after the baptism.

Luke, who in Acts (10:37-38) links God's anointment of Jesus with the Holy Spirit to his baptism, reproduces in his Gospel almost exactly Mark's account of what happened after Jesus' baptism. He changes Mark's account slightly, making the Holy Spirit descend on Jesus while he was praying, not as he was coming out of the water (Luke 3:21-22).

There is an interesting textual variation in one early Greek and several later Latin manuscripts of Luke. Most manuscripts copy Mark in stating that after Jesus' baptism, a voice from heaven said: "*You are my beloved Son*; with you I am well pleased" (Luke 3:22). Yet the other manuscripts have instead this variant of the text: "You are my son; *today I have begotten you*." Bard Ehrman (2007: 158-160), a leading authority on early Christianity, argues that this is what Luke originally wrote and that the text was later changed by copies who did not believe that Jesus became God's son at baptism. The alternative text is clearly more precise in pinpointing the inauguration of Jesus as God's special son to his baptism.

Unlike Mark, Luke has the story of the virginal conception, in which he tells us that Gabriel told Mary that her son Jesus "will be great and will be called the Son of the Most High" (Luke 1:32), and that he "will be called holy — the Son of God" (Luke 1:35). Gabriel's words may be taken to mean that Jesus was the special son of God from the time of his conception, but a more plausible reading is that Luke meant that the angel was mainly conveying future news, and the realization of the special descriptions of Jesus happened after his baptism.

Matthew's nativity story makes Jesus special from the time he was miraculously conceived. This Evangelist states that Mary "was found to be with child from the Holy Spirit" (Matt. 1:18), and that the child she conceived "is from the Holy Spirit" (Matt. 1:20). This surely makes Jesus a special son of God. But it probably also elevates him to divinity in Matthew's eyes. Quoting a prophecy of Isaiah (7:14), he states that the fruit of this miraculous, virginal conception will be called "Emmanuel," which he translates as "God with us" (Matt. 1:23). But in this prophecy, which Matthew quotes here completely out of context (Fatoohi, 2007: 106-107), the name Emmanuel was that of an ordinary, human child whose name stressed God's imminent help in destroying Judea's enemies. This child was not divine. Nevertheless, the way Matthew used Isaiah's prophecy suggests that he believed the child Jesus to be divine. This is in line with his claim that the wise men who came to visit the new born Jesus "worshiped him" (Matt. 2:11). It should be noted, however, that Matthew's account of Jesus' life does not contain any of John's extravagant claims about Jesus' divine attributes. In Matthew's out-of-context application of the Old Testament passage "out of Egypt I called my son" (Matt. 2:15) to Jesus (Fatoohi, 2007: 202), the latter is already a special son of God.

Matthew (3:17) introduces a small change to Mark's story of the baptism of Jesus, making the heavenly voice speak *about* Jesus rather than *to* him: "This is my beloved Son, with whom I am well pleased." The Evangelist (17:1-5) also reproduces Mark's account of the transfiguration which, as pointed out above, does not seem to be particularly significant in stressing Jesus' special status, as this had been established earlier. While the baptism story means that Matthew believed that some kind of elevation to Jesus' status happened then, earlier details in his Gospel clearly shows that he considered Jesus to have been special from birth.

To sum up, Paul thought that Jesus became *the* son of God after his resurrection, Mark believed that this happened after Jesus' baptism, and Matthew reckoned that it happened as early as the time of the conception of Jesus. Luke may have shared Matthew's view, but he is more likely to have adopted Mark's belief. The fundamentally different John believed that Jesus was the special son of God from eternity, although this should not surprise us, as he went as far as deifying Jesus and making him and God almost one.

Theissen and Merz (1999: 554-555) suggest that Jesus became the *only* son of God after the Easter experience. This is clear in the case of Paul. Whether the Evangelists, having accepted that Jesus was *the* son of God, simply reworked when this transformation happened, is difficult to tell.

Paul, Mark, Matthew, Luke, and John have different views about when Jesus became the son of God and the nature of this sonship. In fact, even within the same book it is possible to find passages that are as different as to paint a discrepant picture of this relationship and what the author really wanted to say, raising questions about whether he himself had a clear idea about these elusive theological issues.

Sonship of God, Messiahship, and Miracle Working

The title "son of God" has been linked with another two of Jesus' titles: Christ and king of the Jews. The association with the latter is seen when one enthusiastic believer hails Jesus saying: "Rabbi, you are the Son of God! You are the King of Israel!" (John 1:49).

The Gospels associate the title "son of God" with the "Christ" in four passages. In one passage John tells his readers that he recorded Jesus' miracles so that they believe "that Jesus is the Christ, the Son of God" (John 20:31). Mark (1:1) starts his Gospel with: "The beginning of the gospel of Jesus Christ, the Son of God." When Jesus asks Lazarus' sister whether she believed that the one who believes in him will live even if he dies and that the one who lives and believes in him will never die, she replies "yes, Lord; I believe that you are the Christ, the Son of God, who is coming into the world" (John 11:27). This link between the titles Christ and son of God is also clear in the high priest's accusation of Jesus: "I adjure you by the living God, tell us if you are the Christ, the Son of God" (Matt. 26:63).

The Gospels contain also a number of passages that indicate that the son of God was perceived to be a miracle performer. For instance, reminding Jesus that he was the son of God, the Devil tempted him to turn stones into bread (Matt. 4:3; Luke 4:3). The Devil also tempted Jesus to throw himself from the highest point of the temple and rely on his sonship of God to be saved (Matt. 4:6; Luke 4:9). A demon-possessed man (Mark 5:7; Luke 8:28), who appears as two possessed men in Matthew (8:29); Jesus' disciple who had just witnessed him walk him on the water and still the wind (Matt. 14:33); unclean spirits who saw him (Mark 3:11); and demons that came out of people (Luke

4:41) all called Jesus the "Son of God."

When Jesus stopped the wind, people proclaimed that he was the son of God (Matt. 14:33). Lazarus' sister believed that Jesus could have prevented the death of her brother because he was the son of God (John 11:27). Indeed, Jesus went on to bring Lazarus back to life. Jesus had already revealed that Lazarus' sickness was not fatal but that he was made to die in order for Jesus to miraculously revive him "so that the Son of God may be glorified through it" (John 11:4).

Because the son of God must have miraculous power, the crucified Jesus was sarcastically challenged to prove his sonship of God by coming down from the cross (Matt. 27:40). When the Roman centurion saw the miracles that occurred immediately after Jesus' death, he proclaimed that "truly this man was the Son of God!" (Mark 15:39; also Matt. 27:54).

Even Paul started to teach that Jesus was the son of God after his vision was miraculously restored by one of Jesus' disciples, Ananias (Acts 9:20). John also states that Jesus' miracles proved that he was the Christ and son of God:

> Now Jesus did many other signs in the presence of the disciples, which are not written in this book; but these are written so that you may believe that Jesus is the Christ, the Son of God, and that by believing you may have life in his name. (John 20:30-31)

The implication that performing miracles indicates that the person was the son of God is found in apocryphal gospels also. When a man found out that his possessed son was cured by touching the swaddling clothes of the infant Jesus, he concluded that "perhaps this boy is the son of the living God" (AraIn. 4:21).

The fact is that the link between the title Messiah, sonship of God, and performing miracles is a first century Christian invention that had no origin in Judaism. It is the result of calling Jesus, whom Christians believed to be the Messiah, "son of God" and at the same time portraying him as a miracle worker (Sanders, 1995: 132-133, 160-162).

Sonship of God and Blasphemy

All four Evangelists agree that Jesus' claim to the sonship of God was considered blasphemous by the Jewish authorities (Matt. 26:63-65; Luke 22:70-71; John 10:32-36, 5:16-18):

But he remained silent and made no answer. Again the high priest asked him, "Are you the Christ, the Son of the Blessed?" And Jesus said, "I am, and you will see the Son of Man seated at the right hand of Power, and coming with the clouds of heaven." And the high priest tore his garments and said, "What further witnesses do we need? You have heard his blasphemy. What is your decision?" And they all condemned him as deserving death. (Mark 14:61-64)

The Jews answered him, "We have a law, and according to that law he ought to die because he has made himself the Son of God." (John 19:7)

The rending of one's garment is a Jewish legal requirement for hearing the name of God blasphemed directly or for hearing the blasphemy from the person who heard it first (Sanh. 60a).

One serious historical problem with these passages is that the title "son of God" was not considered to be blasphemous in Judaism (Theissen & Merz, 1999: 464; Vermes, 2005: 29, 101-103). It was not an act of blasphemy or a religious crime to claim to be a son of God. This proclamation could not have been considered a capital offense. This title is used in the Old Testament itself for various people, as we saw in Chapter 3. Pronouncing the four-letter divine name YHVH or speaking disrespectfully about God is blasphemous. This is an instance of pronouncing and abusing the sacrosanct Tetragram from the time of Moses:

Now an Israelite woman's son, whose father was an Egyptian, went out among the people of Israel. And the Israelite woman's son and a man of Israel fought in the camp, and the Israelite woman's son blasphemed the Name, and cursed. Then they brought him to Moses. His mother's name was Shelomith, the daughter of Dibri, of the tribe of Dan. And they put him in custody, till the will of the Lord should be clear to them. Then the Lord spoke to Moses, saying, "Bring out of the camp the one who cursed, and let all who heard him lay their hands on his head, and let all the congregation stone him. And speak to the people of Israel, saying, Whoever curses his God shall bear his sin. Whoever blasphemes the name of the Lord shall surely be put to death. All the congregation shall stone him. The sojourner as well as the native, when he blasphemes the Name, shall be put to death." (Lev. 24:10-16)

According to Vermes (2005: 101), by the start of the 1st century CE blasphemy became specifically linked to pronouncing the divine name YHVH. Rabbinic literature categorically states that "the blasphemer is punished only if he utters [the divine] name" (Sanh. 55b, 56a).

Interestingly, John tells us that Jesus did indeed contest the accusation of blasphemy, although not on the basis of the fact that was known to all that the claim to sonship of God was not blasphemous, but by pointing out that the Jewish scripture used the term "gods" itself for people:

> Jesus answered them, "I have shown you many good works from the Father; for which of them are you going to stone me?" The Jews answered him, "It is not for a good work that we are going to stone you but for blasphemy, because you, being a man, make yourself God." Jesus answered them, "Is it not written in your Law, 'I said, you are gods'? If he called them gods to whom the word of God came — and Scripture cannot be broken — do you say of him whom the Father consecrated and sent into the world, 'You are blaspheming,' because I said, 'I am the Son of God'?" (John 10:32-36)

Jesus argues that as the term "gods" is used figuratively in the scripture, and hence does not break the law, the title "son of God" is similarly metaphorical and cannot be considered blasphemous.

The Old Testament referent in question seems to be Psalms 82:7, which appears to call some gods and sons of God:

> God has taken his place in the divine council; in the midst of the gods he holds judgment: "How long will you judge unjustly and show partiality to the wicked? Selah Give justice to the weak and the fatherless; maintain the right of the afflicted and the destitute. Rescue the weak and the needy; deliver them from the hand of the wicked." They have neither knowledge nor understanding, they walk about in darkness; all the foundations of the earth are shaken. I said, "You are gods, sons of the Most High, all of you; nevertheless, like men you shall die, and fall like any prince." (Ps. 82:1-7)

The Evangelists mistakenly believed that the Jews considered the claim to sonship of God blasphemous. Accordingly, when objecting to the Jewish accusation, Jesus is also seen unaware of the non-historicity of this claim, so he is made to use a different argument to defend himself. In other words, the Gospel authors attributed their later and different understanding of the Jewish concept of "son of God" as referring to divinity to the Jews in Jesus' time. This is an instance of anachronism.

And they (the disbelievers) say: "Allah has taken offspring [to Himself]". Glory be to Him; rather, whatever is in the heavens and the earth is His; all are subservient to Him.

(Qur'an, 2.116)

5

The Qur'an's Rejection of the "Sonship of God"

As we saw in the previous chapter, the Jesus of the New Testament is no normal human being. He is essentially divine. Paul, John, and the writers of other books state this clearly, Matthew seems to suggest it, whereas Mark and Luke are rather ambivalent. Jesus' divinity seems to be the essence of his *unique* sonship of God, even when not spelt out explicitly. This dogma has been central to the Christian faith, yet it is completely rejected by the Qur'an.

Before we study what the Qur'an says about the deification of Jesus, we will discuss its concept of the oneness of God and take a look at how it dealt with Arabia's polytheism.

The Oneness of God

Unlike the God of the New Testament, the image of God in Islam is very clear, and it can be described in a number of simple statements:

(1) There is only one god: "There is no god save Allah" (47.19).

(2) He is the "creator of everything" (6.102).

(3) Before starting the creation, God was alone; eternity is strictly God's: "He is the first and the last" (57.3).

(4) He is the supreme ruler of the universe: "Allah is able to do all things" (5.17); "Allah does what He wishes" (2.253).

(5) God is unique and dissimilar to anything: "There is nothing like Him" (42.11).

(6) He is subtle and out of the reach of anyone's senses: "Vision cannot grasp Him, but He grasps all vision; and He is the Subtle One, the Aware One" (6.103).

(7) Everything and everyone is in submission to Him, whether by choice or by force: "To Him submits whoever is in the heavens and the earth, willingly or unwillingly" (3.83).

Almost all these statements are found in one form or another in the Bible. But the New Testament has other affirmations that blur the meanings of those fundamental statements, or even contradict them. One distinguishing feature of the Qur'an is the absence of such contradictory statements. For instance, while emphasizing that only God is eternal, the Qur'an does not go on elsewhere to qualify this statement by describing someone else as eternal. Similarly, there is a clear-cut ontological separation between God and His creation. No earthly or heavenly being is a god, part of God, or related to God in any form. There is one God, and everyone and everything else is created by Him.

The Qur'an considers any alleged god other than God to be false. It condemns polytheism, i.e. associating gods with Allah, in the strongest terms. It states more than once that assigning partners to God is the gravest sin and the one sin that may not be forgiven (also 4.116):

> Allah does not forgive that anything should be associated with Him, but He forgives anything other than this to whomsoever He pleases; and whoever associates anything with Allah, he devises indeed a great sin. (4.48)

One important difference between the presentations of God in the Qur'an and the New Testament, at least according to the most popular understanding of the latter, is that the God of the Qur'an is *one* whereas the God of the New Testament is *a unity*. Allah is not a number of persons in one, one person in multiple manifestations, one being in different aspects, one in more than one mode, or any such designations that Christianity developed. All that can be said about Him is that He is one. His oneness cannot be broken down into any smaller units or different aspects or forms.

In his effort to show that the Qur'an does not contravene Christian theology, the Methodist minister and professor of comparative religion Geoffrey Parrinder (1995: 137) claims that the Qur'an affirms the unity of God. This suggestion is completely untrue. Under pressure to reconcile contradictory statements in the New Testament, Christian theologians work hard to stress that the concepts of divine oneness and unity are one and the same. The Qur'an rejects this equation, as logic does. The God of the Qur'an is *one, not united.*

According to the Qur'an, God's divinity cannot be shared or divided. Everything and everyone other than God are merely His creation and servants. Spiritual development brings the servant closer to God, but it can never bring him close to divinity. It rather confirms his servanthood. Being nearer to God means getting closer to becoming the perfect Muslim, and the latter is one who has attained complete surrender and submission to God. This is the state in which the individual is no more a servant by compulsion only, but by will also. This means, for instance, that as Jesus was developing spiritually, he was getting closer and closer to attaining the state of perfect servanthood, not divinity.

The Qur'an ascribes to God what it calls *al-Asmā' al-Ḥusnā* (the Beautiful Names) (7.180, 17.110, 59.24): "Allah, there is no god but Him; His are the Beautiful Names" (20.8). These are different attributes that reflect God's different modes of action, including names such as "The Merciful One," "The Majestic One," and "The Creator." Verses 59.22-24 list about 15 of these divine names, with many more found in other parts of the Qur'an. Many verses, such as verse 6.103 above, end with a pair of Beautiful Names. Most scholars count 99 Beautiful Names. In some polytheistic religions, the different actions associated with these names may be assigned to or shared by different gods.

No Offspring of God

The Qur'an's strict monotheism was revealed in the highly polytheistic society of Arabia. The Arabs believed in Allah, but they also believed in other deities (e.g. 13.33, 14.30). They considered Allah to be the chief God and believed in other, lower deities whom they saw as intermediaries who would bring them closer to God:

> It is We who have sent down to you [O Muhammad!] the Book with the truth, therefore worship Allah, making religion pure for Him. (39.2) Pure religion is surely for Allah only, and as for those who take guardians besides Him, [saying] "we do not worship them save that they may bring us nearer to Allah," surely Allah will judge between them about that in which they differ; surely Allah does not guide aright one who is a liar, disbeliever. (39.3)

The Arabs also considered these idols God's offspring (also 18.4-5, 23.84-92):

> And they (the disbelievers) say: "Allah has taken offspring [to Himself]". Glory be to Him; rather, whatever is in the heavens and the earth is His; all are subservient to Him. (2.116)

> They (the disbelievers) say: "Allah has taken offspring [to Himself]". Glory be to Him. He is the Self-sufficient One. His is all that is in the

heavens and all that is in the earth. You have no authority for this [claim]; do you say about Allah what you do not know? (10.68)

These gods were also believed to be females, so they were described as *God's daughters*. Interestingly, the polytheistic society of Arabia considered the female inferior to the male, and the practice of female infanticide was widespread among them until it was prohibited and stopped by Islam (81.8-9). Despite this poor view of females, the Arabs were quite comfortable with making God's offspring females. This contradiction was one argument that the Qur'an used to expose the falsehood of assigning daughters to God, ridiculing the polytheists for wanting males for themselves yet assigning females to God:

> And they (the disbelievers) assign daughters to Allah — glory be to Him — and for themselves what they desire. (16.57) And when one of them is given the news of the birth of a female, his face darkens, and he becomes filled with anger. (16.58) He hides himself from people because of the evil of that which has been announced to him. Shall he keep it with disgrace or bury it [alive] in the dust? Surely evil is what they judge. (16.59)
>
> Or has He taken [to Himself] daughters out of what He creates and preferred you [O you who disbelieve!] with sons? (43.16) And when one of them is given the news of the birth of what he links to God, his face darkens, and he becomes filled with anger. (43.17)
>
> Or has He daughters whereas you have sons? (52.39)

The Qur'an names three of the Arab's female idols, in the context of sarcastically contrasting the miracles that God showed to Prophet Muhammad with the fact that these goddesses could not show anything to their believers:

> He [Prophet Muhammad] has seen of His Lord's greatest signs. (53.18) Have you [O you who disbelieve!] seen Lāt, 'Uzzā, (53.19) and Manāt, the third, the other one? (53.20) So the male is for you and the female is for Him? (53.21) This is an unfair distribution! (53.22)

The Qur'an continues in verses 53.21-22 its sarcastic tone to remind the Arabs that it is unfair of them to attribute to God females and take to themselves males!

The polytheists of Arabia did not restrict the daughtership of God to idols. They believed that the angels, whom they claimed to be females, were also His daughters. The Qur'an rejects that the angels were females and that they were God's daughters:

Those who do not believe in the hereafter call the angels with female names. (53.27) They have no knowledge of that; they follow nothing but conjecture, and surely conjecture can never replace the truth. (53.28)

Has Your Lord [O you who disbelieve!] then preferred for you males and taken [to Himself] females from among the angels? Most surely you utter a grievous saying. (17.40)

And they (the disbelievers) make the angels, who are servants of God, females. Have they witnessed their creation? Their testimony shall be written down and they shall be questioned. (43.19) And they say: "Had God willed, we would not have worshipped them." They have no knowledge of this; they only lie. (43.20)

The idolatrous Arabs also believed that the jinn, whom God created of fire (15.27, 55.15, 7.12, 38.76), have some form of kinship with Him:

So ask them [O Muhammad!]: "Has your Lord daughters whereas they have sons?" (37.149) Or did We create the angels females while they were witnesses? (37.150) It is from their falsehood that they say: (37.151) "Allah has begotten"; and most surely they are liars. (37.152) Has He chosen daughters in preference to sons? (37.153) What is the matter with you? How do you judge [so wrongly]? (37.154) Will you not then reflect? (37.155) Or have you a clear authority? (37.156) Bring your book, if you are truthful. (37.157) And they claim a kinship between Him and the jinn, whereas the jinn know well that they will be brought before Him [on the Day of Resurrection.] (37.158)

Not surprising, then, the people of Arabia worshipped the jinn:

And on the Day [of resurrection] when He will gather them all together, He will say to the angels: "Did these (the disbelievers) worship you?" (34.40) They shall say: "Glory be to You! You are our Guardian, not they. No; they worshipped the jinn; most of them believed in them." (34.41)

We have already quoted verses in which the Qur'an says that the polytheists believed that the angels were God's daughters. One interpretation that the classical exegete aṭ-Ṭabarī (840-922 CE) mentions is that the disbelievers used to see jinn and worship them, and they mistook them for angels. So the angels' reply to God clarifies that the jinn were actively promoting this false partnership with God, perhaps through mediums, whereas the angels never did anything to invite or encourage the polytheists to treat them as divine and worship them. We will later see a similar denial by Jesus when God asks him a similar question about those who worshipped him (p. 70).

In another verse which also denounces the deification of the jinn, the Qur'an argues that the polytheistic claim that some deities were God's offspring, as opposed to being unrelated deities or having any other relationship with Him, can only imply that God fathered them through a relationship with a consort. The concept of *God's offspring* conjures up an image of a god that is very similar to the human being and other creatures:

> And they make the jinn partners with Allah, while He created them; and they attribute to Him sons and daughters, without knowledge; glory be to Him, and highly exalted is He above what they describe. (6.100) He is the Originator of the heavens and the earth! How could He have offspring when He has no consort, and He created everything? And He is the knower of everything. (6.101)

The Qur'an rejects the suggestion that God has a consort, and this rejection is repeated in another verse in words attributed to some Muslim jinn:

> And that exalted be the majesty of our Lord, He has not taken [to Himself] a consort or offspring. (72.3)

Another Qur'anic argument against the claim that God had offspring is that had God had any offspring, Prophet Muhammad himself would have been commanded to worship them, yet Muhammad was sent to call to the worship of the one and only God:

> Say [O Muhammad!]: "If God had offspring, I would have been the first worshipper." (43.81) Glory be to the Lord of the heavens and the earth, the Lord of Throne, above what they describe. (43.82)

The Qur'an also uses the concept of *offspring of God* to reject the divinity of anyone other than God:

> Had Allah wanted to take offspring [to Himself], He would have chosen as He liked from what He has created. Glory be to Him; He is Allah, the One, the Subduer. (39.4)

This verse argues that even if God had wanted to take offspring to Himself, He would have chosen them from His creation. The verse does not mean that it is possible that God could take offspring, but it rhetorically stresses that even in this impossible case God would not have created divine beings, and that such choosing would not have made the chosen creatures divine.

In the same way it stresses that the jinn are a mere creation of God, the Qur'an also clarifies that the angels, whom the polytheists called God's offspring, are no more than pious servants:

> And all creatures in the heavens and in the earth and the angels prostrate themselves to Allah, and they do not show pride. (16.49)

> And they (the disbelievers) say: "God has taken offspring [to Himself]". Glory be to Him. They are rather honored servants. (21.26) They do not precede Him in speech, and they act by His command. (21.27) He knows what is before them and what is behind them; and they do not intercede except for him whom He approves, and they are wary because of their fear of Him. (21.28) And should any of them say: "I am a god besides Him," such a one We reward with hell; thus do We reward the wrongdoers. (21.29)

The Qur'an did not reject the concept of offspring of God only as it was understood by the polytheists of Arabia. It's rejection of this concept is absolute and without any qualification, reservation, or exception (also 18.4, 17.111):

> He to whom belongs the kingdom of the heavens and the earth; and who did not take offspring [to Himself], who has no partner in the sovereignty, and who created everything and ordained for it a measure. (25.2)
>
> And they (the disbelievers) say: "God has taken offspring [to Himself]." (19.88) You [O you who disbelieve!] have made an abominable assertion (19.89) whereby the heavens may almost be rent, the earth cleave asunder, and the mountains fall down in utter ruin, (19.90) that they ascribe offspring to God (19.91). And it is not fit for God to take offspring [to Himself.] (19.92) There is no one in the heavens and the earth but will come to God as a servant. (19.93)
>
> Say [O Muhammad!]: "He, Allah, is One. (112.1) Allah, on whom all depend. (112.2) He has not begotten, nor was he begotten. (112.3) And none is comparable to Him." (112.4)

Not surprisingly, therefore, Christianity's claim that Jesus was God's son is as strongly and comprehensively rebutted in the Qur'an.

Jesus' False "Sonship of God"

Jesus' sonship of God in Christianity is no different from the concept of offspring of God of the polytheists of Arabia:

> He (Jesus) said: "I am Allah's servant. He has given me the Book and has made me a prophet. (19.30) He has made me blessed wherever I may be. He has enjoined upon me prayer and almsgiving so long as I remain alive. (19.31) And [He has made me] kind to my mother and has not made me arrogant or wretched. (19.32) Peace is on me the day I was born, the day I shall die, and the day I shall be raised alive." (19.33) Such was Jesus son of Mary: this is the statement of the truth which they (Christians) dispute. (19.34) Allah would never take offspring [to Himself]. Far exalted is He above this. When He decrees a matter, He says to it only "Be!" and it is. (19.35)

Verses 19.34-35 make it clear that Jesus' alleged sonship of God is as false as any claim of offspring of God. It is the concept that God could have offspring that the Qur'an unreservedly rejects, not the identification of particular beings as God's offspring. Another indirect rebuttal of Jesus', as well as the angel's, divinity is made in this verse:

> And neither would he command you that you should take the angels and the prophets for lords. Would he command you to disbelieve after you have become Muslims? (3.80)

The Arabs were aware of the Christian claim of Jesus' sonship of God, so when they saw Jesus being mentioned and praised in the same book that rejected their daughters of God they argued that Jesus was also considered a son of God:

> And when the son of Mary was cited as an example, your people [O Muhammad!] turned away from him. (43.57) They said: "Are our gods better, or is he?" They raise this only by way of disputation; they are merely a contentious people. (43.58) He is only a servant on whom We bestowed favor and whom We made an example for the Children of Israel. (43.59)

The Qur'an rejects the polytheists' argument because Jesus is not considered a son of God in the Qur'an. On the contrary, it refutes this Christian claim. The Qur'an also stresses that the polytheists knew all too well what the Qur'an says about Jesus, so their argument was not genuine, but contentious.

Contrary to what the New Testament states, it was not Jesus who claimed to be the son of God. Jesus' sonship of God is seen by most Christians as a form of divinity, yet Jesus never claimed to be divine. He stressed that he was human, and that he was sent by God to deliver a message. His followers later split into different factions and distorted his teachings, and his original message was lost:

> When Jesus came with clear proofs, he said: "I have come to you with Wisdom, and to make plain some of what you have disagreed on. So keep your duty to Allah, and obey me. (43.63) Allah is my Lord and your Lord. So worship Him. This is a straight way." (43.64) But factions from among them differed. Woe to those who do wrong from the torment of a painful day. (43.65)

It is rather irrelevant, according to the Qur'an, what terminology is used to express Jesus' divinity and his relationship to God. This terminology, the discussion of which has occupied Christian theologians since the formative days of Christianity after Jesus' departure, would not change the fact that the very claim that Jesus is divine removes the distinction between him and God. In Qur'anic theology, divinity sums up the fundamental difference between God, on the one hand, and everything and everyone else, on the other. To say that someone is divine yet try to differentiate him from God is a logical fallacy and a meaningless exercise. Indeed, no matter how theologians express Jesus' divinity, he and God end up being treated equally and interchangeably. Any prayer that can be made to God can be equally addressed to Jesus. To attribute divinity to Jesus, therefore, is to make him equal to God:

> They have indeed disbelieved those who say: "Allah is the Messiah son of Mary." Say [O Muhammad!]: "Who then can do anything against Allah if He had willed to destroy the Messiah son of Mary, his mother, and everyone on earth?" Allah's is the kingdom of the heavens and the earth and all that is between them. He creates what He wills. Allah is able to do all things. (5.17) And the Jews and the Christians say: "We are the sons of Allah and His beloved ones." Say [O Muhammad!]: "Why does He then chastise you for your faults? No, you are human beings from among those whom He has created; He forgives whom He pleases and chastises whom He pleases." And Allah's is the kingdom of the heavens and the earth and what is between them, and to Him is the eventual coming. (5.18)

Some Christian scholars have wrongly claimed that the Qur'an rejects the concept of sonship of God because it implies procreation. What the Qur'an therefore actually denies, they suggest, is a corrupt interpretation of the New Testament's concept of Jesus' sonship of God which does not imply any act of procreation (Cragg, 1999: 189-207; Parrinder, 1995: 136-137). It is common among critics of the Qur'an to claim that its rejection of certain concepts and practices represents a response to particular groups that held a corrupt understanding of the Jewish and/or Christian scriptures, or reflects a misunderstanding by the author of the Qur'an, who is supposed to be Muhammad, of what the scriptures say.

The Qur'an rejects that God was involved in any procreation but, as I have already explained, it rejects the divinity of Jesus regardless of how this divinity is explained — whether it implies procreation or not. Interestingly, none of the verses (6.101, 72.3, 37.152, 112.3) that deny that God had a consort or begot offspring occurs in the context of talking about Jesus' sonship of God. The Qur'an's rejection is not directed at an outlandish interpretation of the Christian scriptures or derives from a misunderstanding of these writings. Christian writings present Jesus' sonship of God as a form of divinity, and this is why this sonship is rejected by the Qur'an. Verse 5.18 above sheds clear light on this issue.

The Qur'an mentions the historical fact that the Jews, and later the Christians, called themselves sons of God. Significantly, the Qur'an differentiates between this *mass* sonship of God and Jesus' *unique* sonship of the Divine. While the latter sonship is condemned as imbuing Jesus with divinity, the former is not considered blasphemous. The Qur'an recognizes that the Jews' and Christians' claims to sonship of God are not a claim to any form of divinity, and that they only signify close servanthood to God. So its rejection of these claims is only directed at their implication that God treats the Jews and Christians preferentially. The Qur'an refutes this implication by pointing out that the followers of these religions are treated in the same way others are. Should a Jew or Christian fail in his duty toward God, this believer would be punished accordingly, and the "son of God" tag would do nothing to protect him from that punishment. The verse then reminds all that the Jews and Christians are merely human beings created by God, and that what applies to humans in general applies to the followers of these religions.

This condemnation of the claim that the Jews and Christians are the sons of God is reminiscent of other verses that criticize the self-image of the Jews, which Christians later borrowed, as the chosen people of God:

> And they [the People of the Book] say: "No one shall enter paradise except those who are Jews or Christians." These are [merely] their desires. Say [O Muhammad!]: "Produce your proof if you are truthful." (2.111) Yes, whoever becomes a Muslim (surrenders himself) to Allah and is a doer of good, his reward is with his Lord, and there is no fear for them nor shall they grieve. (2.112)

The Qur'an states that people are not judged by how they label themselves or are labeled by others, but by their beliefs and deeds (also 5.69):

> Those who believe, the Jews, the Christians, and the Sabaeans — whoever believe in Allah and the Last day and does good — they shall have their reward from their Lord, and there is no fear for them, nor shall they grieve. (2.62)

He commands all people not to try and praise and commend themselves as He knows who is pious and who is not:

So do not ascribe purity to yourselves; He knows best those who are pious to God. (53.32)

In another verse that condemns describing Jesus as the son of God, the Qur'an also anathematizes the claim by some Jews that a certain 'Uzayr was the son of God:

> The Jews say: "'Uzayr is the son of Allah," and the Christians say: "The Messiah is the son of Allah." That is a saying from their mouths, imitating the saying of the disbelievers of old. May Allah fight them! How deluded they are! (9.30) They have taken their rabbis and monks as lords besides Allah, and so they treated the Messiah son of Mary, although they were not commanded to worship other than One God; there is no God save Him. Far exalted is He above their attribution of partners to Him! (9.31)

Exegetes usually identify 'Uzayr with the Prophet Ezra of the Old Testament. This is a possible identification, but there is no evidence to support it. Verse 9.30 does not accuse *all Jews* of considering 'Uzayr the son of God. The Qur'an uses the definite name of a group to refer to some of them. For instance, "the Qur'an states that "the Jews," meaning *some Jews*, killed prophets and tampered with God's word. Similarly, "the people" is used to mean "some people" (e.g. 2.13), and so on. So "the Jews" in verse 9.30 means *some Jews*. The fact that this belief is restricted to some Jews only explains why, even though the Jews and Israelites are mentioned much more than the Christians in the Qur'an, it is mentioned only once whereas the sonship of God of Jesus is rejected several times.

As we have already seen in Chapter 3, Judaism did not use the title son of God to imply divinity. Verse 9.30 makes it clear that 'Uzayr's sonship of God was taken to mean that he was divine, as it was the case with Jesus, so clearly the reference is to a heterodox belief among a small Jewish group or cult, which probably lived in Arabia at the time of Prophet Muhammad. The older disbelievers that the verse mentions are people who lived before the Jews and the Christians and believed, as the latter later did, in forms of sonship of God. The concept of sonship of God can be found in various ancient civilizations.

The reference to the Jews and Christians taking their rabbis and monks, respectively, as lords besides God does not mean that they considered them divine. It rather highlights the unconditional surrender to what these clerics taught, even when their teachings went against God's. It is reported that Prophet Muhammad was asked about this verse by a Christian who pointed out that the Christians did not worship their monks. The Prophet replied that the Christians followed their monks who permitted things that God had declared unlawful and prohibited things that God had made lawful, and this was the equivalent of worshiping them, because they were allowed to overrule God's law.

The Qur'an separates the condemnation of the claims of 'Uzayr's and Jesus' sonship of God from its indictment of treating the rabbis and monks as lords. Note that the verse uses the term "lords" not "gods." Also, verse 9.31 mentions the treatment of the rabbis and monks as lords separately from the fact that Jesus was also treated so. Jesus' lordship is derived from the belief in his divinity, whereas treating rabbis and monks as lords only referred to the fact that people followed them blindly. Indeed, two verses later in the same chapter the Qur'an exposes the fact that many rabbis and monks had conned people and turned them away from the right path:

> O you who believe! Many of the rabbis and monks eat away the property of people falsely and turn [people] away from Allah's way; and [as for] those who hoard up gold and silver and do not spend it in Allah's way, to them give [O Muhammad!] tidings of a painful chastisement [on the Day of Judgment.] (9.34)

The Qur'an does not reject the lordship of the rabbis and monks just to replace it with lordship of Muhammad. No human being should treat another as a god or even as a lord who can change or override the commands of the ultimate Lord, God:

> Say [O Muhammad!]: "O People of the Book! Come to an equitable agreement between us and you: we shall not serve any other than Allah, we shall not associate anything with Him, and we shall not take from among each other lords besides Allah." But if they turn away, then say: "Bear witness that we are Muslims." (3.64)

Another misconception advocated by some Christian scholars (e.g. Parrinder, 1995: 137) is that the Qur'an does not reject Jesus' sonship of God absolutely, but only denies adoptionism, i.e. the belief that God adopted Jesus at some point as His son (pp. 48-52). Bishop Kenneth Cragg shares this view, and he argues that the Qur'an's rebuttal of adoptionism is no indication of its rejection of the doctrine of the Incarnation, i.e. that God took a human form in the person of Jesus:

> Where the Qur'an remonstrates against Christian faith in Jesus' Incarnation, what it in fact accuses is not Incarnation but adoptionism, itself a heresy. However, it serves little purpose for

Christians to "exploit" this and argue from it that the Qur'an mistakes what it is rejecting and, therefore, might be claimed not to reject what Christians believe. This would be both barren and contentious, a disservice both to fact and to right intention. The operative term is *ittikhāth* (cf. 17.111, 19.35, 19.92, 39.4). "God's not taking to himself a son" is a conviction Christians share. The phrase does not describe, and so does not in itself deny, what the Gospel means by "the Word made flesh" and the Creed by "the only begotten Son." (Cragg, 1999: 38-39)

I have already presented substantial evidence that the Qur'an rejects Jesus' divinity, whether this is presented as procreation, adoptionism, incarnation, or any other form. I would like to add two more points here about Cragg's wrong link of the Arabic verb *yattakhith* (takes to himself) to adoptionism. **First**, the Qur'an's rejection of Jesus' sonship of God is not always associated with the use of the verb *yattakhith* or God's *taking of a son to Himself*. We have already seen verses where this sonship is denied without any qualification and where there is no room to suggest that what is being rejected is any one particular form of deification. **Second**, scholars such as Cragg ignore the fact that *yattakhith* is used with many nouns, not only "son," that its general meaning is "considers" or "treats as," and that it has no explicit or implicit emphasis on the *time* of occurrence of the action it refers to. There are numerous verses to show this (e.g. 2.67, 2.80, 3.28, 4.89). One example is the Qur'an's statement that "Allah took (*ittakhatha*) Abraham as a close friend" (4.125). The verb clearly does not imply any act of adoption of Abraham by God.

Furthermore, the Qur'an uses the verb *ittakhatha* with the rejection of the concept of offspring of God, not only the Jesus' sonship. The verses that are particularly interesting here are those where the verb *yattakhith* is used specifically when talking about the taking of other than Jesus as alleged gods. When referring to the sin of the Jews who disobeyed Moses and worshipped a calf, the Qur'an uses the verb *yattakhith* to mean "take as a god" (2.92, 4.153, 7.148, 7.152). The verb *yattakhith* here cannot mean "adopt." The same applies to these verses (also 19.81, 21.21, 21.24):

And Allah has said: "Do not take (*tattakhithū*) two gods; He is only one God; so be fearful of Me." (16.51)

These, our people, have taken (*ittakhathū*) gods besides Him; why do they not produce a clear authority in their support? Who is then more wrong than he who forges a lie against Allah? (18.15)

In each and every one of these verses, the verb *yattakhith* is used to mean "take" and appears in the context of rejecting considering something or someone as a god. No sense of "adopt" is implied or even possible. Moreover, in verse 5.116 the verb *yattakhith* is used in the context of denying the divinity of not only Jesus, but also his mother Mary, so clearly it cannot mean "adopt":

> And when Allah said: "O Jesus son of Mary! Did you say to people: 'Take me (*ittakhithūnī*) and my mother for two gods besides Allah?'" He said: "Glory be to You! I could never say what I have no right to say. If I have said it, then You know it. You know what is in my mind, but I do not know what is in Your mind. You know all unseen things. (5.116) I never said to them anything other than what You commanded me: 'worship Allah, my and your Lord.' I was a witness over them while I was among them, and when You took me You were the watcher over them. You are a witness over all things. (5.117) If You punish them, they are Your servants; and if You forgive them, You are the Invincible, the Wise." (5.118)

This dialog happened after God took Jesus to live in a heavenly place and rescued him from the attempt to get him crucified (Fatoohi, 2007: 445-452). Jesus lived until his *middle age*. The Arabic term in verses 3.46 and 5.110 that I have translated as "middle-aged" is *kahl*. This term is taken by exegetes and linguists to denote the period after youth and before old age, with almost all identifying it as covering the late thirties and forties and when the person has grown grey hair. According to the highly regarded lexicon *al-Qāmūs al-Muḥīṭ* of the well-known linguist al-Fayrūz Ābādī, *kahl* means "someone with grey hair and a respectable appearance, or someone who is over thirty or thirty four up to fifty one." I am inclined to think that Jesus was still a young man when he left the earth, so he might have lived some 20-30 years in the new, non-earthly place before he died. This dialog, therefore, does not mean that Jesus and his mother were already being treated as divine before he was taken to heaven. It is far more likely that the distortion of Jesus' teachings began when he was no longer around to confirm his real message and counter the attempts to turn him and his mother into gods.

It was probably Paul who sowed the seeds of the deification of Jesus and it was among his communities of pagan converts that this distorted teaching gained momentum and flourished and ultimately influenced even some Jewish converts. Unlike Judaism, Roman paganism accommodated the concept of the divinity of human beings. Most scholars also think that the deification of Jesus happened after he was gone. Larry Hurtado (2003: 131) stresses that "the Gospels confirm that the worship of Jesus in 'post-Easter' Christian circles represents a significant development beyond the sorts of homage given to Jesus during his ministry." It was not the historical Jesus who taught people to worship him. Considering the historical context of Jesus' teachings, and even taking into account the Gospel accounts, his deification must be considered as a development that Jesus had no involvement in and happened after him:

> To state something that hardly requires argumentation, in the setting of first-century Jewish Palestinian society, the profound commitment to the exclusive worship of the one God, and an equally profound antipathy toward deification of humans, make it most improbable that either his followers or those Jews who approached him for help offered what they would have intended as "worship" of him as divine. Though gentiles may have been more comfortable with reverencing human figures as divine, any who might have offered such reverence to Jesus in supplicating him for his healing and exorcistic powers would have been regarded as misguided. To be sure, in that cultural setting, it would have been fully appropriate to make reverential gestures toward someone regarded as a respected teacher or a source of desperately-needed help. But the far more intense devotion to Jesus that characterized early Christian circles so amazingly early was not simply the continuation of the pattern of homage given to the historical Jesus, and it cannot be accounted for adequately by reference to Jesus' ministry. (Hurtado, 2003: 144-145)

To put it in a stark way, modern scholars have concluded what the Qur'an revealed 14 centuries ago, that Jesus taught that he was a man and that his message and image were changed after him as pagan beliefs turned him into a god. I will discuss in more detail Paul's role in defining Christianity in Chapter 7.

Verse 5.116 gives another clear confirmation that Jesus never claimed to be divine, which means he never claimed to be the son of God. The verse also mentions the fact that many Christians turned Mary also into an object of worship, i.e. made her divine like her son. The worship of Mary or "Mariolatry" is also a concept that is foreign to Jesus' teachings. In verse 5.116 Jesus stresses that he never commanded people to consider him or his mother divine. Jesus tells God that he only taught what God ordered him to teach, which is to worship God, who is his and everyone's Lord.

The Qur'an also stresses Jesus' human nature through the metronymic title "son of Mary." Semitic people are called after their fathers, so in addition to emphasizing the fact that Jesus had no father, this metronymic is intended to deny any suggestion that he was a son of God. This description of Jesus occurs 23 times in the

Qur'an. Only the name Jesus occurs more — 25 times. Interestingly, Jesus is only once called "son of Mary" in the whole of the New Testament: "'Is not this the carpenter, the son of Mary and brother of James and Joses and Judas and Simon? And are not his sisters here with us?' And they took offense at him" (Mark 6:3). However, the New Testament frequently uses the significant title "son of man." I will later argue that Jesus used this title to stress his human nature and rebuff the suggestion that he was the son of God or any attribution of divinity to him (pp. 81-83).

There is no reason to suggest that the title "son of man" is directly linked to the metronymic "son of Mary." The latter is always used by God in the Qur'an. There is no instance of Jesus referring to himself as "son of Mary." It is difficult to think of a suitable use by Jesus of this title anyway. On the other hand, almost all occurrences of "son of man" in the New Testament are found in sayings of Jesus. My conclusion is that God, as well as people, called Jesus after his mother, "son of Mary," and that Jesus used the periphrastic expression "son of man" to refer to himself. Both are intended to stress Jesus' human nature and refute claims that he was divine.

6

Son of Man

In the Gospels, Jesus frequently refers to himself as the "son of Man." We will see in this chapter how this expression, which sets a marked contrast with the title "son of God," is another indication that Jesus rejected the attempts to deify him.

The term "son of man" translates the Aramaic *bar nasha* or *bar nash* and the Hebrew *ben 'adam*, which literally means "son of Adam." In the Old Testament, it is found once in Job, twice in Daniel, and over 90 times in Ezekiel. In the much smaller text of the Gospels, this expression occurs at a much higher frequency — namely, 82 times. It occurs 14 times in Mark, 30 in Matthew, 25 in Luke, and 13 in John. In the rest of the New Testament it is found only twice in Revelation in quotations from the Old Testament, once in Acts, and once in Hebrews.

The Unhistorical Link Between "Son of Man" and "Messiah"

Scholars have been arguing about the exact meaning of "son of Man." One modern scholar described the failure of scholars to reach any major consensus as "one of the great embarrassments for modern historical scholarship" (Dunn, 2003, 725). More specifically, some have maintained that it was a pre-Christian Jewish title that denoted the eschatological figure of the Messiah and this is how they understand Jesus' repeated use of the term. The majority of scholars reject this view. Those who take "son of Man" to be a Jewish designation for the Messiah cite three main textual sources in support of their theory: 1 Enoch 37-71, 4 Ezra 13, and Daniel 7:13.

1 Enoch ascribes itself to the 7th patriarch in Genesis, but it is considered as a pseudepigraphical work whose author is unknown. Its complete version survives in an Ethiopic translation which is believed to have been made as late as the 6th century CE, but its earliest extant manuscript comes from as late as the 16th century. The book is a conglomeration of a number of works of different origins, and it has

been rated by some scholars as one of the hundred worst books (Campbell, 1947: 148). The chapters that interest us here are 37-71 — the *Parables* or *Similitudes*. They talk about an eschatological figure who is described as "the righteous one," "the elect one," and "the Messiah." He is linked to Jesus because he is also called "the son of man." Nevertheless, the *Parables* cannot be proved to be pre-Christian. In fact, many scholars believe that it was written by Christians, probably around the end of the 1st century or in the 2nd, so it does not reflect pre-Christian Jewish beliefs (Longenecker, 1969: 152-153; Sanders, 1995: 246, 308).

The second source, 4 Ezra 13, survives in a number of translations of the Greek version. The latter and its Semitic source have both been lost. This source does not actually use the term "son of man," but talks about an eschatological *man* who comes from the sea and with the clouds of heaven. He destroys the multitudes that start a war against him. Like 1 Enoch 37-71, this book is also believed to have been written late in the 1st century (Longenecker, 1969: 153).

Unlike the first two sources, the Old Testament Book of Daniel is certainly pre-Christian. This is how Prophet Daniel describes what he saw in one of his visionary dreams:

> I saw in the night visions, and behold, with the clouds of heaven there came one *like a son of man*, and he came to the Ancient of Days and was presented before him. And to him was given dominion and glory and a kingdom, that all peoples, nations, and languages should serve him; his dominion is an everlasting dominion, which shall not pass away, and his kingdom one that shall not be destroyed. (Dan. 7:13-14)

The son of man in this passage has been taken to signify an eschatological individual, giving the term a titular function. It was interpreted as a reference to *the Messiah*. I find this interpretation of Daniel's "son of man" misguided. **First**, this is the only instance of its 96 appearances in the Old Testament where the term is claimed to be used as a title and to have messianic eschatological connotations. **Second**, this expression appears again in the next chapter in Daniel in an angel's speech to the prophet where it simply means "human" or "mortal" (Dan. 8:17). **Third**, Daniel 7:13 does not actually describe the heavenly figure as "a son of man." To the contrary, by describing him as being "*like* a son of man" the author is pointing out that he is *not* a son of man (Campbell, 1947: 148). Daniel meant that although the supernatural figure he saw looked like a son of man, he knew that he was not. That figure was not a human being, so he could not have been the Messiah.

So there is no textual evidence on the existence of the concept of the "son of man" as an apocalyptic figure in pre-Christian Jewish thought. The expression "son of man" does not appear as a title in Daniel, the Parables, or 4 Ezra 13 (Bock, 1991: 111; Campbell, 1947; Longenecker, 1969, 1975). This is how the Christian professor Frederick Bruce puts it:

> "[T]he Son of man" was not a current title, whether for the Messiah or for any other eschatological figure. When Jewish thinkers devised a title for the figure who is brought to the Ancient of Days, it was not the Son of man but Anani (the "cloud-man"). There does not appear to have been any existing concept of "the Son of man" which Jesus could have taken over and used either to identify himself or to denote a being distinct from himself. (Bruce, 1982: 60)

Researchers who insist that "son of man" existed as a title in pre-Christian Judaism have had to assume that the three texts above use "son of man" as a title and then conclude that the existence of this titular use means that the expression must have been established before Jesus (e.g. Horbury, 1985). This is actually more of a clever wording of the assumption than an argument based on evidence.

The term "Messiah" is applied in the Old Testament to *historical* not *future* figures. Furthermore, in its 39 occurrences in the Old Testament, the title "Messiah" is applied to a number of different individuals who occupied three different positions: king, priest, and prophet. To quote from my book *The Mystery of the Messiah*:

> Scholars believe that after the overthrowing of the last Davidic ruler of Judea, Zedekiah, by Nebuchadnezzar II in 586 BCE, the concept of "anointed king" started to be understood to mean "*the* Messiah" — the final Jewish king who would free them from foreign control, reestablish the Jewish kingdom, and return to Israel its lost glory (Vermes, 2000: 177). The Jews started to give more attention to the figure of a Messiah particularly after the fall of the Maccabean dynasty (165-63 BCE), coming under Roman rule, and the usurping of Judea by Herod the Great (40-4 BCE) and his family who were backed by the heathen Romans. This waiting for the Messiah grew stronger in the years leading to the two Jewish revolts against the Roman in 66-70 and 132-135 CE. The several salvational Davidic figures started to be seen as one eschatological savior: "The Messiah." The prominence of the Messiah in the Jewish faith grew to the extent that the influential Jewish theologian and philosopher Maimonides (1135-1204 CE) made the belief in the Messiah and waiting for his coming the 12th of his 13 principles of Jewish faith. (Fatoohi, 2009: 11)

However, I have also pointed out a number of serious flaws in this explanation of the development of the concept of one salvational, eschatological Messiah. Relying on the fact that the Qur'an talks about *one Messiah* only and considering related historical facts about this term, I have concluded the following:

> The unique Qur'anic Messiah leads me to conclude that the concept of *the Messiah* is of divine origin, having been inspired to prophets who were sent to the people of Israel. But human intervention distorted this concept over the centuries. Influenced by their troubled history, national aspirations, and misunderstanding of what it meant to be God's chosen people, Jewish theologians and writers developed a Jewish-centric image of the Messiah. This image was held by those who later became the first Christians, but after accepting that Jesus was the Messiah they had to redraw some of its details to reflect the history of Jesus. The image of the Messiah in Christian writings is based on what the Christians believed Jesus *actually* did and said, combined with some *expectations* about the future, so it differs from the portrait of the Jewish Messiah. The Qur'anic Messiah differs from the Jewish and Christian Messiahs, being presented as a highly elevated prophet of God. The Qur'an has preserved the concept of this unique Messiah as it was originally revealed to Israelite prophets, in contrast to the changed versions found in Jewish and Christian sources. (Fatoohi, 2009: 14)

The New Testament, which was written in that turbulent period of Jewish history, must have been influenced by that atmosphere. Indeed, there are passages that have clearly been modeled on Daniel 7:13, showing the son of man coming with or on the clouds from heaven (also Mark 13:26; Matt. 26:64; Luke 21:27):

> And you will see the Son of Man seated at the right hand of Power, and coming with the clouds of heaven. (Mark 14:62)

> Then will appear in heaven the sign of the Son of Man, and then all the tribes of the earth will mourn, and they will see the Son of Man coming on the clouds of heaven with power and great glory. (Matt. 24:30)

> Then I looked, and behold, a white cloud, and seated on the cloud one like a son of man, with a golden crown on his head, and a sharp sickle in his hand. (Rev. 14:14)

Note Revelation's use of Daniel's expression "*like* a son of man."

There are other appearances of the term "son of man" in the Gospels that *may* be taken to reflect the Evangelists' association of this term with the Messiah. For instance, these passages present the "son of man" as a victorious heavenly End-time figure who commands the angels (also Matt. 16:27, 25:31; Luke 9:26, 12:8):

> For whoever is ashamed of me and of my words in this adulterous and sinful generation, of him will the Son of Man also be ashamed when he comes in the glory of his Father with the holy angels. (Mark 8:38)
>
> The Son of Man will send his angels, and they will gather out of his kingdom all causes of sin and all law-breakers. (Matt. 13:41)
>
> Truly, truly, I say to you, you will see heaven opened, and the angels of God ascending and descending on the Son of Man. (John 1:51)

The son of man is also associated with the forgiving of sins and healing (e.g. Matt. 9:6; Luke 5:24):

> "But that you may know that the Son of Man has authority on earth to forgive sins" — he said to the paralytic — "I say to you, rise, pick up your bed, and go home." And he rose and immediately picked up his bed and went out before them all, so that they were all amazed and glorified God, saying, "We never saw anything like this!" (Mark 2:10-12)

John applies many of the attributes of his special son of God to the son of man. The son of man came from God and returned to Him: "No one has ascended into heaven except he who descended from heaven, the Son of Man" (John 3:13). He also has Jesus say to his disciples: "Then what if you were to see the Son of Man ascending to where he was before?" (John 6:62). The son of man has authority to judge, and believing in him gives eternal life (also John 6:27):

> For as the Father has life in himself, so he has granted the Son also to have life in himself. And he has given him authority to execute judgment, because he is the Son of Man. (John 5:26-27).
>
> "And as Moses lifted up the serpent in the wilderness, so must the Son of Man be lifted up, that whoever believes in him may have eternal life. "For God so loved the world, that he gave his only Son, that whoever believes in him should not perish but have eternal life. (John 3:14-16)

If the Gospel authors or their sources did mean *at times* to use "son of man" as a *title* for the Messiah, which is far from clear, then I think that would have been the result of the combination of the facts that Jesus used this term frequently to refer to himself, the Evangelists' belief that Jesus was the Messiah, and their influence by a certain interpretation of Daniel 7:13. What is clear, however, is that most of the time the expression did not have any Messianic function, as it was not a Jewish designation for the Messiah. In explaining the titular, religious use of the expression "son of man" in the Gospel of John, Vermes notes the following about the religious use of this phrase in Jewish literature:

> From the completion of the Book of Daniel in the 160s BC to the time of the destruction of Jerusalem in AD 70 there is no attestation in extant Jewish literature of the use of "son of Man" as describing a religious function. However, in the decades following the first Jewish war against Rome which ended in AD 70, that is during the period of the composition of the Gospels, we possess independent literary evidence in which such a man-like figure is portrayed as a heavenly Messiah (4 Ezra 13), or a superterrestrial final Judge (Parables of Enoch, or 1 Enoch 37-71). (Vermes, 2000: 39)

There are other facts and arguments that support our earlier conclusion, which Vermes confirms, that there is no evidence that the expression "son of man" was a recognized title for the Messiah before Jesus. **First**, neither before nor after Jesus did the term "son of man" ever gain popularity as a designation for the Messiah, despite the fact that Jesus applies it to himself in the Gospels over 80 times and more explicitly and directly than any other title, including "Christ." It is almost completely absent in the New Testament outside the Gospels, appearing only four times (Acts 7:56; Heb. 2:6; Rev. 1:13, 14:14. It is never used by Paul. Furthermore, its possible use as a title for an eschatological figure remained limited to a very small number of sources, including the two instances in Revelation.

Second, the term "son of God" appears 82 times in 79 passages in the Gospels, excluding Matthew 18:11 which is dropped from some more recent translations of the New Testament because it is missing from the most reliable early Greek manuscripts. Significantly, unlike the title "son of God" which occurs on the lips of a number of different people and spiritual beings, almost all occurrences of "son of man" in the Gospels are found in Jesus' sayings. The only exception is John 12:34, but even here people mention it in the context of asking Jesus about what he meant by saying that the "son of man" would be lifted up. Had "son of man" been an established title before Jesus we would have seen it in the Gospels used by people to refer to Jesus, not only used by him.

Third, hearing this expression did not have any unusual effect on people. Had it been a special title of some prominence, let alone an epithet of the Messiah, it would have invoked certain reactions. Nothing of the sort is reported.

Jesus' Use of the Term "Son of Man"

But is it possible that it was Jesus who introduced "son of man" as a *special title*? The answer is no, because there is no indication anywhere in the Gospels that people needed Jesus to explain to them the term "son of man." At no point were Jesus' listeners puzzled by the expression or unable to understand it. Had Jesus introduced the expression as a special appellation he would have needed to explain it to people whenever he used it or they would have asked him about it.

So what was the meaning of "son of man" which was clear enough not to require explaining by Jesus or enquiring by people? This is what Vermes — who shares the scholarly consensus that Jesus' main language was Aramaic, like the Jews of Palestine — has to say:

> Outside the New Testament, "son of man" is most commonly employed in the Aramaic language by Jews either as a noun ("a man/the man"), or as the indefinite pronoun ("one/someone"), but neither of these usages is applicable to the Synoptic Gospels. Furthermore, in the Galilean dialect of Aramaic spoken by Jesus, "son of man" sometimes appears in a monologue or dialogue as a circumlocutional reference to the speaker himself. It is not unlike the English figure of speech, "yours truly," used in place of "I." For example, "Who is the author of this splendid piece?" or "Who is responsible for this horror?" may produce the modest or shamefaced reply, "Yours truly." The purpose of such a periphrastic style was to camouflage something fatal dreaded by the speaker or something that would sound boastful if directly asserted. So one would say in Aramaic, *the son of man* is going to die, or *the son of man* is about to become king, rather than *I* will die, or *I* will be proclaimed king. (Vermes, 2000: 38-39)

Vermes notes that, unlike the Synoptics which use "son of man" for "I," John combines this circumlocutional use with a titular one. This should not surprise us, as John is far more focused on theology than the Synoptic Gospels. John was also developed later than the other Gospels and is thus more distant from Jesus, so we can safely conclude that Jesus used the expression "son of man" in the sense of "I." Also, as this term was not connected to any particular imagery in the minds of Jesus' audiences, they must have simply taken it to mean "I," i.e. as a reference to Jesus himself.

This is one example in which Jesus clearly uses "son of man" for the personal pronoun "I" in the same passage:

> For whoever is ashamed of *me* and of my words in this adulterous and sinful generation, of him will the *Son of Man* also be ashamed when he comes in the glory of his Father with the holy angels. (Mark 8:38)

Matthew's wording of a passage that is found also in Mark and Luke is particularly instructive of how the Evangelists understood "son of man":

> And Jesus went on with his disciples to the villages of Caesarea Philippi. And on the way he asked his disciples, "Who do people say that *I* am?" (Mark 8:27)
>
> Now it happened that as he was praying alone, the disciples were with him. And he asked them, "Who do the crowds say that *I* am?" (Luke 9:18)
>
> Now when Jesus came into the district of Caesarea Philippi, he asked his disciples, "Who do people say that the *Son of Man* is?" (Matt. 16:13)

Matthew replaced the "I" in Mark with "son of man," whereas Luke retained the original. Here is another example where the term "Son of Man" in Luke appears as "I" in Matthew:

> So everyone who acknowledges me before men, *I* also will acknowledge before my Father who is in heaven. (Matt. 10:32)
>
> Everyone who acknowledges me before men, the *Son of Man* also will acknowledge before the angels of God. (Luke 12:8)

These examples show that the Evangelists treated the expression "son of man" as a circumlocution for "I" (compare also Mark 8:38, Matt. 10:33, and Luke 9:26; Mark 10:45, Matt. 20:28, and Luke 22:27).

Theissen and Merz would object to this conclusion, pointing out that the association of the expression "son of man" with Jesus could not have been derived from everyday language only. They ask: "Why should an expression which in principle everyone could use and which could mean anyone be so closely associated with Jesus that it was retained even after Easter, when for Christians Jesus had already long since been more than a man?" They argue that Jesus must have persistently used the everyday term to turn it into a title for himself, with one possible reason being Jesus' attempt to counteract specific expectations that were being associated with him:

> Jesus must have used the everyday expression emphatically so that it could become his "title" — say by using it to correct excessive expectations; other people might expect miracles of him, other people might hope that he was the stronger one expected since John the Baptist, others might throng after him — but as a correction of such expectations he emphasized his human status as "son of man" (Mark 2:10; Matt. 11:18, 8:20). So among other things the expression became a christological title because Jesus opposed it to christological expectations and thus made it a mysterious honorific title first for his followers. In the Gospel texts after they have been subjected to redaction, this corrective function of the term "Son of Man" can still be

detected: Peter confesses Jesus as the Messiah, but Jesus answers by prophesying the suffering of the Son of Man (Mark 8:29). Jesus is asked about his messiahship before the Sanhedrin, but replies with a saying about the Son of Man (14:61.) (Theissen & Merz, 1999: 550)

I completely agree that it must have been Jesus who used the expression "son of man," and I also accept that Jesus did so in order to countervail excessive beliefs about him. I do not agree, however, that the target of his action was Christological or miracle expectations:

(1) The phrase "son of man" does nothing other than emphasize the human nature of Jesus, as Theissen and Merz note, yet the Messiah was expected to be a human being anyway, albeit with special authority and powers. Those powers were not linked to any superhuman origin, so they could not be offset by reminding people that the Christ was human.

(2) Jesus did proclaim to be the Messiah, but he set the right expectations by stressing what his messiahship meant. In the simplest terms, it was a call for people to obey God. He clearly and robustly rejected any attempt by people to assign to his messianic role any political function, as in his rebuke to his testers to "render to Caesar the things that are Caesar's, and to God the things that are God's" (Mark 12:17; Matt. 22:21; Luke 20:25).

(3) The expectations of miracles from him could not have been the target of his persistent use of the expression "son of man," because he did perform miracles!

The expression "son of man," which emphasized Jesus' human nature, could have had only one target to counteract: claims or expectations of Jesus' divinity. By frequently using this phrase periphrastically, Jesus stressed his human nature and rejected claims about his divinity that had either already started to circulate or, more likely, he expected to appear at some point after him. As has been pointed out, this expression "could not be understood in the Greek world otherwise than as referring simply to the humanity of Jesus." Furthermore, the early Church fathers saw in this title a reference to the human nature of Jesus' descent. So "from the Apostolic Fathers to the present, the title has come to be regarded in the dogmatic theology of the Church as but the converse of the title Son of God. But in the early Church it was not so" (Longenecker, 1969: 157). So even those who recognized and promoted Jesus' divinity accepted that the title "son of man" denoted his humanity. One such modern Christian theologian notes that this title "obviously speaks of [Jesus'] humanity and His identity with humankind" (Witmer, 1998: 51).

The tension between the terms "son of man" and "son of God" may be seen in Matthew's adaptation of one of Mark's passages:

> And Jesus went on with his disciples to the villages of Caesarea Philippi. And on the way he asked his disciples, "Who do people say that *I* am?" And they told him, "John the Baptist; and others say, Elijah; and others, one of the prophets." And he asked them, "But who do you say that I am?" Peter answered him, "You are the Christ." (Mark 8:27-29)
>
> Now when Jesus came into the district of Caesarea Philippi, he asked his disciples, "Who do people say that the *Son of Man* is?" And they said, "Some say John the Baptist, others say Elijah, and others Jeremiah or one of the prophets." He said to them, "But who do you say that I am?" Simon Peter replied, "You are the Christ, the *Son of the living God.*" (Matt. 16:13-16)

Significantly, Matthew's replacement of "I" with the expression "Son of Man" is followed by the addition of the epithet "Son of the living God." This suggests that the author was aware of what "Son of Man" meant to people so he went out of his way to stress Jesus' sonship of God also.

The relentless attempts to change Jesus' status from man to God after he had gone, which succeeded at the end, fully justified every action that Jesus took to stress his human nature. The determination to promote Jesus' divinity was so strong that, ironically, the refutative expression "son of man" was itself used, as in John, to ascribe divine attributes to Jesus! The circumlocutional expression "son of man" was turned into a title and used at times exactly like the epithet "son of God" which was applied to Jesus in a special way. Jesus would not have replaced the term "God" in "son of God" with "man" to coin a new appellation just to use both titles interchangeably!

Of course, not all "son of man" sayings are authentic. Probably many of them were made up and others were changed to convey whatever messages the Evangelists wanted to pass to their readers. For instance, I do not believe that Jesus talked about coming back to this world after departing it, be it on the clouds or in any other way. I have discussed the subject of Jesus' second coming elsewhere (Fatoohi, 2007: 467-491). Also, any use of "son of man" other than periphrastically to confirm his human nature and deny having any divine attributes is inauthentic.

There are a number of reasons that make me believe that Jesus did indeed use the expression "son of man." **First**, it is used in many of his reported sayings. **Second**, it is used exclusively by him. **Third**, it did not play an important or prominent role in the development of Christian thought, so there is no reason to believe that it was introduced after him to serve a particular theological function. **Fourth**, it is particularly suitable for averting and rejecting his deification. In his rebuttal of the suggestion that all "son of man" sayings are inauthentic, one scholar has rightly pointed out that this view makes incomprehensible "why the early Church should have created the title for Jesus, never to use it except on his own lips as a self-designation in the Gospels" (Kazen, 2007: 163).

Given that Jesus frequently called himself the "son of man" to preempt and reject any attempt to ascribe divine attributes to him, how likely is it that he could have referred to God as *his father*, thus calling himself indirectly "son of God"? Since at the time of Jesus the Jewish concept of "sonship of God" had no divine connotation, it may be argued that Jesus could have called God his father. But the counter, and probably stronger, argument is that given that Jesus realized that he was going to be deified, which is why he repeatedly referred to himself as the "son of man," he would have recognized that a claim to sonship of God might be misunderstood or abused by others to suggest he was divine, so it is unlikely that he called God his father. Interestingly, while all instances of "son of man" occur in Jesus' sayings, the title "son of God" is applied to Jesus only by others in the Synoptics; only John, who was particularly interested in promoting a certain theology and used history as a tool in this endeavor, puts it on Jesus' lips (e.g. John 10:36)!

I should finally mention that my conclusions above clearly refute the suggestion of some Muslim scholars that "son of man" was a title that Jesus used for Prophet Muhammad (Dawud, 1994: 223-263).

They have indeed disbelieved those who say: "Allah is the Messiah son of Mary." Say [O Muhammad!]: "Who then can do anything against Allah if He had willed to destroy the Messiah son of Mary, his mother, and everyone on earth?" Allah's is the kingdom of the heavens and the earth and all that is between them. He creates what He wills. Allah is able to do all things.

(Qur'an, 5.17)

Part III

A Divine Theology for a Non-Divine Jesus

7. Pauline Christianity 87
    Paul's Unhistorical Jesus 87
    The Doctrine of the Atonement 92
    Johannine Theology: The Ultimate Fruit of Pauline Christianity 93
    The Heterogeneous Scriptural Sources of Christianity 95

8. The Trinity 99
    The Development of the Doctrine of the Trinity 100
    The Fallacy of the Trinity 103

9. Jesus: A Man Created by God and a God Created by Humans 107

He (Jesus) is only a servant on whom We bestowed favor and whom We made an example for the Children of Israel.

(Qur'an, 43.59)

7

Pauline Christianity

Christianity is named after Jesus Christ, and his teachings played a role in its development. But it was Paul's teachings that ultimately decided what this religion came to be. Christianity, which developed after Jesus, has very little resemblance to the historical teachings of this great master. As we explained earlier (pp. 23-25), Jesus' mission was to confirm the verity of Moses' message, bring the good news about the coming of Prophet Muhammad, and modify certain aspects of the Mosaic law. Jesus never claimed to be other than a man sent by God like Moses and other prophets before him, but it was Paul who elevated Jesus to divinity, and that divine Jesus became ultimately the Jesus that Christianity preached.

Paul's Unhistorical Jesus

Significantly, Paul does concede in one of his epistles that *his* Jesus was not the same Jesus that was being preached by others:

> For if someone comes and proclaims another Jesus than the one we proclaimed, or if you receive a different spirit from the one you received, or if you accept a different gospel from the one you accepted, you put up with it readily enough. Indeed, I consider that I am not in the least inferior to these super-apostles. Even if I am unskilled in speaking, I am not so in knowledge; indeed, in every way we have made this plain to you in all things. (2 Cor. 11:4-6)

Equally significant is Paul's description of those rivals as being "super-apostles." They would have been seen so and he would have found himself on the defensive only if these apostles had something he could not claim to himself. This is likely to be the fact that those apostles either accompanied Jesus or at least were present where Jesus lived, so they could claim credibility that Paul could not. Paul declared his faith in Jesus years after he had gone. It is telling that Paul's writings show no interest in or knowledge of Jesus' history, focusing only on the theological significance of the crucifixion and resurrection and making a passing mention of the Last Supper

(Fatoohi, 2008a: 93).

Paul openly declared that his knowledge did not come from any scripture or followers of Jesus but rather through direct revelation: "The gospel that was preached by me is not man's gospel. For I did not receive it from any man, nor was I taught it, but I received it through a revelation of Jesus Christ" (Gal. 1:11-12). As some of Paul's teachings are not found anywhere else in the New Testament, making his teachings core Christian theology is nothing short of giving him at least an equal role to Jesus.

Furthermore, Paul's credibility rests wholly on his claim that Jesus appeared to him (Acts 9:3-8, 22:6-10, 26:13-18). Yet even if Paul did indeed experience something usual or even paranormal on his way to Damascus to persecute Christians, that does not justify accepting his teachings as core Christianity, if the latter is taken to mean the religion that Jesus taught rather than accurately seen as a religion that developed well after Jesus had gone. History was never going to have much to say about Jesus' alleged appearance to Paul, but we know that what Paul ended up teaching has nothing to do with what Jesus preached.

Paul was open about the fact that he had no contact whatsoever with the historical Jesus, claiming that his contact with the divine/spiritual Jesus told him all he needed to know about the truth of Jesus. He clearly believed that he knew Jesus more than anybody else. Paul's letters show him as an absolutely determined, single-minded person, so it is highly unlikely that he was not influenced by others in his decision to deify Jesus.

Jesus' Jewish followers in Palestine could not have started the move to deify him and his mother. Judaism is a strictly monotheistic religion, so even if someone wanted to promote Jesus' divinity, he would have met very little acceptance and strong opposition.

Paul, however, was in a different position, because he focused his missionary efforts on Roman Gentiles outside Jewish Palestine. Presenting Jesus as divine would have looked completely logical and natural for pagan converts. Paul and ultimately Christianity gave the Jewish title "son of God" a strong divine connotation that was never part of its Jewish origin. Christianity used the title "son of God" as another way of saying "God." But the concept of *son of a god* was well-known and accepted in the Hellenistic culture. The unique and supernatural qualities of heroes and their extraordinary lives were explained in terms of divinity, and this divinity at times came in the form of sonship of a god. Gods physically fathered such heroes. They had a divine father and a human mother, but there were exceptions where the mother was a goddess and the father a man. Ancient Greek sons of gods include the athlete Theagenes, whose father, the god Heracles, appeared to Theagenes' mother in the form of her husband and impregnated her; the 6th century BCE philosopher Pythagoras who was fathered by Apollo; the 5th-4th century BCE philosopher Plato whose father was the god Phoebus; Alexander the Great who was fathered by a god who took the form of a snake and slept with his mother; the sage Apollonius of Tyana whose father was Zeus; and Emperor Augustus whose mother is said to have claimed that he was fathered by the god Apollo (for more details, see Miller, 2003: 133-153). Gentile converts accepted Jesus' divine image very easily, and might have even needed it to believe in him.

Bible scholar Robert Miller thinks that Jesus, like the previous sons of gods, was considered a divine son of God in order to explain his extraordinary life. However, while the Jews at the time of Jesus were influenced by the Hellenistic culture, they were under much bigger influence from their own cultural heritage. Specifically, their religion remained completely monotheistic. Jesus' sonship of God cannot be explained as being the result of the influence of the Hellenistic culture on Palestinian Jewish believers in Jesus. It should be noted that both the Old and New Testaments have stories of prominent holy figures whose lives were clearly extraordinary and involved supernatural events, yet they were not called sons of God, and certainly not considered divine — for example, Abraham in the Old Testament and Zechariah in the New Testament.

Paul did not know much about Jesus' life. He certainly did not think it is worth mentioning in his writings, if he knew anything about it. It may be argued that he might have come up with the concept that Jesus was divine because he believed in his resurrection. But this conversion, according to Paul himself, happened only after he miraculously saw Jesus, so it looks like any interpretation of the significance of the resurrection would have been a consequence rather than an initiator of faith.

Miller also believes that the story of Mary's virginal conception of Jesus was made up because it was required by the title "son of God." This suggestion also ignores completely the Jewish influence on the authors of Matthew and Luke, in which this story appears. Luke is written from a Gentile perspective, and for this and other reasons the author is often considered to have been a heathen convert. But Matthew is written from a Jewish perspective so the author is considered to have been a Jew. Miller's suggestion tries to explain parts of the Gospel of Matthew as if they were written in complete isolation from the author's main culture. **First**, the concept of miraculous conception and birth is applied in both the Old and New Testaments to human beings who were not called sons of God, although none of these was conceived without a father. For instance, the Old Testament talks about the miraculous conception of Isaac (Gen. 18:10-11), and the New Testament has the story of John the Baptist (Luke 1:13-19). In both cases the parents were too old to have a child. But neither of the two sons was called a son of God, so the story of their miraculous conceptions could not have been inspired by this title. **Second**, the Old Testament contains stories of holy figures who lived extraordinary lives, and the Jewish title son of God was thus applicable to them, yet they were conceived and born naturally, without any miracle. One instance is King David who was anointed as a Messiah by prophet Samuel as instructed by God (1 Sam. 16:12-13), established a united kingdom for all Israelites, and was spoken to by God (2 Sam. 23:3). I have discussed the subject of the virginal conception in detail elsewhere (Fatoohi, 2007: 99-119).

It is interesting to note the different positions of the main Christian sources and the Qur'an about Jesus' virginal conception and sonship of God: Matthew and Luke mention both the virginal conception and the sonship of God; Paul, Mark, and John talk only about Jesus' sonship of God; whereas the Qur'an talks about the virginal conception but rejects the sonship of God. The Qur'an's rejection of Jesus' sonship of God reflects a fundamental difference between its theology and Christian theologies.

Paul was of a Jewish monotheistic background, so why would he promote the pagan concept of man-god? One obvious possibility is that he rejected his monotheistic roots and simply believed that Jesus was divine for whatever reason. Another possibility, which is not necessarily mutually exclusive with the previous one, is that he wanted to align the new religion with the expectations of the target pagan audience of his missionary work. We know, for instance, that Paul did not hesitate in dropping circumcision as a requirement from

Gentile converts to the religion he was preaching (e.g. Rom. 2:25-29, 3:29-30; 1 Cor. 7:18-19). The Book of Acts and Paul's letters recount sharp disputes that Paul had with prominent Jerusalemite Christians because of his abolishment of certain legal requirements, which he clearly did to convert as many Gentiles as possible. Around sixteen years after his conversion, Paul and his companion Barnabas traveled from Antioch to Jerusalem to meet the apostles and elders to sort out the disagreement that his teachings had created. A heated debate about the observance of Moses' law was followed by a respected James deciding that the Gentiles can be exempted from circumcision. James also said that the Gentiles should be sent a letter telling them that they should simply "abstain from what has been sacrificed to idols, and from blood, and from what has been strangled, and from sexual immorality" (Acts 15:29). If the Gentile converts avoided these four, the letter stated, they would be fine. Paul won. More details on Jesus' attitude toward the law can be found in my book *The Mystery Of The Historical Jesus* (pp. 377-388).

There is a lot of say about this exchange between Paul and his opponents and the amazing reduction of the law to four prohibitions only. It shows, for instance, that Paul had taken the liberty of teaching a form of Christianity that was his own creation. But the main observation that concerns us here is that this account shows how Paul was keen on sacrificing sacred elements of the Jewish religion in order to win over pagan converts to the religion of Jesus that he was preaching.

But how could Paul's missionary efforts in various parts of the Roman empire succeed in changing Jesus' original message in Judea? The reason is that, contrary to the belief of most Christians which is based on the Gospel accounts, Jesus had a very small group of followers in his homeland. One major reason for this is that the Messiah he claimed to be was very different from the one that the Jews had been hoping for for centuries. The destruction of the northern state of Israel in the 7th century BCE by the Assyrians and the devastating attack on the southern state of Judea in the 6th century BCE by the Babylonians started a dark period of occupation of the Jews by foreign, heathen states. This resulted in the concept of the awaited Messiah being changed from referring to a reformist prophet to a military leader who would liberate the Jews and restore the lost Glory of ancient Israel. This reformation of a distorted ethnocentric concept of the Messiah ensured that Jesus was never going to be popular and attract a sizeable following:

> Jesus confirmed that he was the Christ, but he also disapproved of what the concept of the Christ had become. For him, the Christ was a spiritual prophet and teacher, not someone with a political or secular agenda. The Messiah was a reformer who would lay down again the foundations of the religion of Abraham, Jacob, Moses, Aaron, and all other Israelite prophets. This rather unpopular image of the Messiah is probably why only a small minority of the Jews, not many thousands as suggested by the Gospels, believed in and followed him, even though he was a miracle worker. The majority of the Jews chose to remain faithful to the prevailing Jewish concept of the Messiah. (Fatoohi, 2009: 39-40)

Jesus' miracles helped him to attract followers and those who needed his miracles. But the change he promoted was too different from what the public wanted and they preferred the distorted dream to the truth that he preached. Jesus had therefore a small following, and this made changing the essence of his message, including turning him into a god, possible.

The Doctrine of the Atonement

The divine Jesus that Paul created has, naturally, theological implications. One major theological contribution that Paul has made to Christianity is his introduction of the doctrine of the Atonement. The latter, the Incarnation, and the Trinity represent the three most influential doctrines in Christianity. The Atonement and the Trinity were both derived from the deification of Jesus, i.e. the most fundamental doctrine of the Incarnation.

The Atonement denotes the role of the death and resurrection of Jesus in bringing about the reconciliation between God and man after Adam's sin (Rom. 3:21-26, 5:6-21). Sin represents death, so by making his son die and bringing him back to life, God gave people the opportunity of salvation. As Paul put it in his first letter to the Christians of Corinth in Greece: "For as in Adam all die, so also in Christ shall all be made alive" (1 Cor. 15:22). Paul taught that the Atonement was so fundamental to Christianity that he told his fellow Christians: "If Christ has not been raised, your faith is futile and you are still in your sins" (1 Cor. 15:17).

Amazingly, despite its fundamental position in Christian theology, the doctrine of the Atonement is not found in any of the Gospels which are presented as collections of Jesus' sayings and works. There is not even a passing mention by Jesus to this supposedly most fundamental doctrine that represents his whole mission in life, death, and resurrection. Even when Jesus tells his disciples about the suffering he was expecting, the Gospel writers do not attribute to him a single word indicating that this suffering has a vicarious function (Mark 8:31, 9:12; Matt. 16:21, 17:12; Luke 9:22, 17:25, 22:15, 24:26, 24:46)!

The Qur'an rejects completely the concept of the Atonement. **First**, the Qur'an rejects the concept of original sin, which states that Adam committed a sin which all his descendants were made to inherit and thus be born in a state of sinfulness. Yet the concept of original sin forms the basis of Paul's Atonement, even though original sin started to develop as a doctrine in the 2nd century before it reached the summit of its power at the hands of Bishop of Hippo St. Augustine (354-430 CE). **Second**, the salvational role that a prophet plays is achieved by guiding his followers to genuine beliefs and practices. Whether an individual goes to hell or paradise is determined by his behavior, not by any action taken on his behalf by anyone else, including a prophet. The reader may consult my book *The Mystery of the Crucifixion* for a more detailed analysis of the doctrine of the Atonement (Fatoohi, 2008a: pp. 57-65) and its refutation in the Qur'an (pp. 125-132).

Jesus' sacrifice replaced the Mosaic role as the necessary route to salvation. Paul did not promote a complete abrogation of the law, but one letter that used to be attributed to him in the past said that Jesus' sacrifice resulted in "abolishing the law of commandments expressed in ordinances" (Eph. 2:15). The almost complete absence of the law from the Christian life is a testimony to Paul's success.

Furthermore, the concepts of a suffering Messiah and a Messiah who rescues people through his death and resurrection do not exist in Judaism. Both are Christian inventions that have no roots in history.

Johannine Theology: The Ultimate Fruit of Pauline Christianity

The Johannine image of the divine Jesus is not found in the other three Gospels. None of the latter describes Jesus as an incarnate of the Word, portrays him as the primordial light, suggests that he always existed, states that Jesus and the father are in each other, makes them one and the same, or calls Jesus God. None of this is found in the Synoptics. The Johannine deification of Jesus would have appalled any Jew as indisputable blasphemy, and would have been seen so even by Mark, Matthew, and Luke. Although these authors took Jesus' special sonship of God to reflect an intimate relationship with God that may imply some form of divinity, John's divine Jesus remains alien to them. The Gospel of John is so different from the other Gospels that had it failed to make it into the canon, the Jesus that Christianity has been promoting would have been completely different. But despite its major differences from the Synoptics, John's Gospel succeeded in making its unique theology central to Christian belief.

It is generally accepted that John wrote his Gospel to assert the divinity of Jesus — a highly contentious view in early Christianity. But the Gospel of John was written as late as the 2nd century CE, so it must have been influenced by earlier oral and written traditions. When we talk about "Johannine" theology we should not imply teachings that *started* by the author of the Gospel of John. This description only underlines certain theological views that this particular and relatively late Gospel *propagated*.

The earlier of the Gospels, Mark, was written around 70 CE — at least a decade or two after Paul's letters. Matthew and Luke are usually dated to around 80-90 and 70-100 CE, respectively. The Gospel of John is the latest of the four. It was written over half a century after Paul's letters. John represents the extreme to which the Pauline theological seed of the deification of Jesus was taken. This Gospel captures the outcome of decades of theological development of Paul's representation of Jesus as divine by various people. John offers details of the divine Jesus that are not even hinted at in Paul's writings. It is an advanced piece of highly creative theology.

We do not have a detailed, step-by-step history of the development of the Johannine theology from Paul's writings, as we do not have earlier documents that can help us trace that. But we know that over the decades after Jesus a number of images of this man were being developed by different theologians. The substantial differences between the Synoptics and John show that there were very different strands of oral and written traditions available to those authors to pick from. We also know that almost nothing of this goes back to

Jesus himself.

The competition to draw Jesus' image continued unabated for centuries, and from that relatively late period we have a plethora of written sources. The early history of Christianity and the Church is a history of conflicts between competing concepts, doctrines, and theologies.

The development of the Johannine theology should be credited to Gentile converts to Christianity. The Christian divine son of God was clearly influenced by the same concept that was part of the Hellenistic culture. Those who were born Christians, so were not influenced by Judaism even if their parents were originally Jews, could also have contributed to this theology.

The Heterogeneous Scriptural Sources of Christianity

The differences between the scriptural books of Christianity reflect a very significant fact about this religion which we need to discuss.

Christianity is named after Jesus Christ and is attributed to him, but it is not defined only by his words and acts, which are reported in the four Gospels. A number of unknown authors of its holy books have defined this religion. The apostle Paul has played a particularly influential role in this definition.

The collection of Christianity's holy books — the New Testament — contains another 23 books written by a number of different authors, although they are said to have been guided spiritually when writing those books. The Book of Acts is attributed to the same author of one of the Gospels, Luke. A number of other authors are responsible for 9 books: Hebrews, James, First Peter, Second Peter, First John, Second John, Third John, Jude, and Revelation.

The remaining 13, particularly influential, books are attributed to the apostle Paul, as each starts with his name. But only 7 letters of these epistles, modern scholars agree, were written by Paul: Romans, Philippians, Galatians, Philemon, First Corinthians, Second Corinthians, and First Thessalonians. The latter is regarded as the earlier book of the New Testament and is dated to around 50 CE. Of the remaining six letters — Ephesians, Colossians, Second Thessalonians, First Timothy, Second Timothy, and Titus — some are subject to scholarly disagreement while others have almost all agreed were not written by Paul. Nevertheless, this modern classification of these 13 letters is almost irrelevant to the history of Christianity. For many centuries all letters were promoted by the Church as authentic Pauline epistles and have therefore played a substantial role in defining Christian theology.

The credibility of these 27 books, and ultimately the religion they represent, depends very much on the credibility of their authors. Yet the identities of most of these authors are completely unknown and their histories cannot be traced. The same argument can also be made about Judaism, whose scriptures consist of writings by various authors of whom very little if anything is known. Christianity accepts the Old Testament books also as holy scripture, so these also can be considered as sources of this religion. But Christian theologians have restricted the role of the Jewish books to providing support to the theology propagated by the New Testament books.

This is a fundamental difference between Islam and Christianity and Judaism. The credibility of the Islamic faith rests solely on the credibility of the Qur'an and the prophethood of Muhammad. Muhammad claimed to have received the Qur'an from God and that neither he nor anyone else contributed to it. The Qur'an is the only divine text in Islam. No spiritual experience of any other Muslim figure, ancient or modern, constitutes part of the faith, and no other writings have a claim to inerrability. This applies even to the words attributed to Muhammad, known as *aḥādīth*, or the special group of sayings known as *aḥādīth qudsiyyah* or "divine sayings" that are believed to represent divine revelation expressed in Muhammad's words. These were reported down the centuries by numerous people. The fact that Muhammad's prophethood is the only foundation of Islam is manifested in the fact that the following two verses form the declaration of faith in Islam: "There is no god save Allah" (37.35, 47.19) and "Muhammad is the messenger of Allah" (48.29).

Western scholars have questioned whether the Qur'an we have today is the same Qur'an that Muhammad taught and they have suggested that the process of compiling it was far from perfect. But even this extreme claim, which is challenged by many, is completely different from the criticism above of the New Testament and the Old Testament. Whether any ancient holy book was compiled, copied, and disseminated faithfully or not is a question that can be asked about any book. The point I make above is that Islam is based on one book that is attributed to God and one man who claimed to be God's Prophet, whereas Christianity and Judaism are each based on a large number of books by different, unknown authors each of whom is presumed to have been guided by God.

I have ignored in the discussion of this section how Christians came to believe in their holy books or the "canon." The reality is that early Christian groups and theologians differed on what books were holy. Actually, the earliest Christian mention that the New Testament consists of the 27 books that we have today is as late as 367 CE. It is in a letter from Athanasius, the bishop of Alexandria, to the Egyptian churches. I have discussed the question of the authenticity of the canon versus apocrypha elsewhere (Fatoohi, 2007: 23-28).

The Messiah, Jesus son of Mary, was only a messenger of Allah, His Word that He sent to Mary, and a Spirit from Him [that He sent]. So believe in Allah and His messengers, and do not say "Three." Desist, it is better for you! Allah is one God. Far exalted is He above having offspring. His is all that is in the heavens and all that is in the earth.

(Qur'an, 4.171)

8

The Trinity

The New Testament, as well as other early Christian writings, contains passages that promote monotheism and others that ascribe to Jesus divine attributes, and passages that stress the distinctness of the Father and the Son and others that fuse the two. These contradictory writings served as a fertile environment for the development of a number of conflicting and ambiguous doctrines. This confused theological language reflects more influence by the Roman understanding of divinity than by Jewish monotheism. Even if only the Gospel of John is considered and all other canonical and apocryphal Christian books are ignored, this single book would still provide too many discrepant, confusing, and vague statements to allow a harmonious, coherent, and clear picture of Jesus.

Soon after Jesus was gone, some Christian converts started to debate whether he was a mere human being, with some ascribing to the man divine attributes and others making him essentially a god. Whether Paul borrowed his views from someone else or developed them himself, which is far more likely, it was he who established the divinity of Jesus in Christianity. There were other views that reflected genuinely Jesus' message and presented him as a man only, but Paul's Jesus prevailed over the historical one.

The heated debates about the nature of Jesus that continued over decades and centuries resulted in the development of a number of different concepts and doctrines. All of these derived from the most fundamental doctrine of the Incarnation. Adoptionism, for instance, stated that the Son joined the Father in divinity at some point. Docetism claimed that Jesus had only an appearance and did not have a physical body. Theologians interested in Jesus' divinity tackled issues such as whether the Son and the Holy Spirit were always present with the Father, the nature of the relationship between the three, and whether they were equal. Ultimately, the majority of Christians were led to accept the answers to these questions that the doctrine of the Trinity provided. But this doctrine itself was developed over centuries of controversies, and different theologians have understood and explained it differently.

The Development of the Doctrine of the Trinity

Tertullian of Carthage (ca. 155- after 220), who introduced the term "Trinity" from the Latin "trinitas" (three or triad), taught the concept of one God in three persons: the Father, the Son, and the Holy Spirit. These three are distinct, but not separate. Because these three persons are not separate or divided, God is one, not three. Tertullian's Trinity is, therefore, a form of monotheism not tritheism.

Another form of the Trinity, which Tertullian considered heresy is known as "Sabellianism," after the 3rd century theologian Sabellius. "Modalism," as it is also known, states that God is one in three aspects or modes. In this version, the Father, the Son, and the Holy Spirit are not distinct persons but different manifestations of the Godhead. Accordingly, it was God who suffered on the cross, hence this view is also called "patripassionism," which is derived from the Latin words for "father" and "suffer." Like Tertullian's version, this form of the Trinity equally claims to promote the oneness of God.

In the 4th century a major controversy broke out between Bishop Alexander of Alexandria, Egypt, and the Alexandrian priest and theologian Arius. The former believed that the Father and the Son were both eternal and of equal status. Arius believed the Son was not eternal and was inferior to the father. The Arians, while still advocating the divinity of the Son, insisted that there is substantial difference between the Father and the Son.

The spread of this controversy prompted Emperor Constantine to arrange and oversee the first Ecumenical Council, which was held in Nicea in 325 CE. The convening bishops, whose number has been put by different sources between 250 and 318, released the first decree that addressed the status of the Father and the Son and their relationship, but it only affirmed the belief in the Holy Spirit. This decree was not the result of as much consensus as Constantine's influence and pressure. Having been given the choice of signing to the decree or being sent into exile, Arius and his allies chose the latter. The wording of the decree was vague and open to different interpretations, but it was still clear enough to reject Arianism:

> We believe in one God, the Father, almighty,
> maker of all things visible and invisible;
> And in one Lord Jesus Christ, the Son of God,

begotten from the Father, only-begotten, that is,
from the substance of the Father, God from God,
light from light, true God from true God,
begotten not made, of one substance with the Father,
through whom all things came into being,
things in heaven and things on earth,
Who because of us men and because of our salvation
came down and became incarnate, becoming man,
suffered and rose again on the third day, ascended to the heavens,
will come to judge the living and the dead;
And in the Holy Spirit.
But as for those who say, there was when He was not,
and, before being born He was not,
and that He came into existence out of nothing,
or who assert that the Son of God is of a different
hypostasis or substance, or is subject to alteration or
change — these the Catholic and apostolic Church anathematises.
(Kelly, 1999: 215-216)

In the following half a century the debates and disagreements continued unabated, and when the second Ecumenical Council was convened in Constantinople in 381, the convening 150 bishops revised the creed and gave it its final shape, which now addressed the status of the Holy Spirit also and, thus, the doctrine of the Trinity:

We believe in one God, the Father, almighty,
maker **of heaven and earth**, of all things visible and invisible;
And in one Lord Jesus Christ, the **only-begotten** Son of God,
begotten from the Father **before all ages**, light from light,
true God from true God, begotten not made,
of one substance with the Father, through whom all things came into existence,
Who because of us men and because of our salvation came down from heaven,
and was incarnate **from the Holy Spirit and the Virgin Mary** and became man,
and was crucified for us under Pontius Pilate,
and suffered **and was buried**, and rose again on the third day
according to the Scriptures and ascended to heaven,
and sits on the right hand of the Father,
and will come again with glory to judge living and dead,
of whose kingdom there will be no end;
And in the Holy Spirit, the Lord and life-giver,
who proceeds from the Father, who with the Father and the Son is together
worshipped and together glorified, who spoke through the prophets;
in one holy Catholic and apostolic Church.
We confess one baptism to the remission of sins; we look forward to the resurrection of the dead and the life of the world to come. Amen.
(Kelly, 1999: 297-298)

The deletions from the Nicean formulary and the additions, which

I have highlighted in bold above, are instructive in understanding issues that were at the center of the debates between Christian theologians.

Some doubts have been raised about whether this revision was made in the 381 council (Kelly, 1999: 305-331). It is first mentioned as an official formulary in the Chalcedon Council in 451 CE where the convening bishops clearly believed that the creed had been composed and ratified in Constantinople.

The Niceno-Constantinopolitan Creed, as it has become known, was accepted by both the Eastern and Western Churches. The history leading to the formulation of this authoritative formulary, however, was full of controversy, and the consensus that was finally achieved conceals many bitter battles and much struggle between prominent Churchmen who held opposing views. For a detailed study of the history of the development of this creed, the reader may like to see *Early Christian Creeds* (Kelly, 1999).

The development of the Trinity was simply a consequence of the introduction of the more fundamental doctrine of the Incarnation. This is how one prominent scholar explains it:

> The doctrine of the Trinity was developed as an interpretive framework to secure the prior doctrine of the deity of Christ. That is to say, if Jesus Christ was God incarnate, but if throughout the period of his earthly life God was also at work sustaining the universe, receiving prayer and otherwise acting outside the person of the historical Jesus, it follows that the Godhead is as least two-fold, namely Father and Son. This was the essential expansion or complication of monotheism required by the belief in divine incarnation. And when the Spirit of God, attested to in religious experience is added, we have a Trinity. (Hick, 1997: 7)

Jesus was not the only holy figure that Christianity deified. His mother Mary was also later transformed into an object of worship in a doctrine known as Mariolatry or the "worship of Mary," even though there is nothing to support this exaltation of Mary's status in the New Testament. Among the titles Christians conferred on Mary are "Mother of God" and "Queen of Heaven." Mariolatry led to the introduction of dogmas such as the "immaculate conception," by Pope Pius IX in 1854, which states that Mary was free of the original sin from birth, like Jesus. Another dogma is the "assumption of Mary," by Pope Pius XII in 1950, which teaches that after her death, Mary's soul and body were taken to heaven.

The Fallacy of the Trinity

Unsurprisingly, the Qur'an denounces explicitly the Trinity doctrine:

> O People of the Book! Commit no excesses in your religion or utter anything concerning Allah but the truth. The Messiah, Jesus son of Mary, was only a messenger of Allah, His Word that He sent to Mary, and a Spirit from Him [that He sent]. So believe in Allah and His messengers, and *do not say "Three."* Desist, it is better for you! *Allah is one God.* Far exalted is He above having offspring. His is all that is in the heavens and all that is in the earth. Allah is sufficient a disposer of affairs. (4.171) The Messiah would never scorn to be a servant to Allah, nor would the angels who are nearest to Allah. As for those who scorn His service and are arrogantly proud, He shall gather them all to Himself to answer. (4.172)

The Trinity is presented as being contrary to Jesus' servanthood to God. The New Testament portrays Jesus as being both divine and a servant of the Divine. The Qur'an's argument rejects this duality as an impossibility. Verse 4.171 also clearly considers the Trinity as a form of tritheism not monotheism. Put differently, the concept that God is a unity is not the same as God is one. The next verse then stresses that Jesus and the nearest angels have completely accepted their servanthood to God.

The second rejection of the doctrine of Trinity occurs in this set of verses:

> Surely they disbelieve those who say: "Allah is the Messiah son of Mary." The Messiah himself said: "O Children of Israel! Worship Allah, my Lord and your Lord. Whoever joins other gods with Allah, for him Allah has forbidden paradise. His abode is the Fire. The evildoers shall have no helpers." (5.72) Surely *they disbelieve those who say: "Allah is one of three." There is only one God.* If they will not desist from what they say, a painful torment shall befall the disbelievers among them. (5.73) Will they not rather repent to Allah and seek His forgiveness? Allah is forgiving, merciful. (5.74) *The Messiah son of Mary was no other than a messenger before whom similar messengers passed away, and his mother was a saintly woman. They used to eat food.* See how We make the revelations clear to them, and see how they are deluded! (5.75) Say [O Muhammad!]: "Will you worship besides Allah that which has no power to harm or benefit you?" Allah is the Hearer, the Knower. (5.76) Say: "O People of the Book! Commit no excesses of falsehood in your religion, and do not follow the vain desires of folk of old who erred, led many astray, and strayed from the even path. (5.77) Those who disbelieved from among the Children of Israel were cursed by the tongue of David and of Jesus son of Mary. That was because they disobeyed and used to transgress. (5.78)

After rejecting the Trinity (5.73), the Qur'an goes on in verse 5.75 to stress that Jesus was only a messenger like many others who lived and died in the past, so Jesus was no special case. It also emphasizes that Mary was merely a righteous woman, in clear reference to her elevation by many Christians to a divine or semi divine status.

Some scholars have suggested that the Qur'an mistakenly takes the Trinity to be the Father, the Mother, and the Son, i.e. the *divine family*. This conclusion is probably influenced by the fact that in verses 5.72-75 the denouncement of deification of Mary, as well as that of Jesus, occurs after the rejection of the Trinity. I agree with Parrinder (1995: 135) that there is actually nothing in the Qur'an to suggest this interpretation. The weakness of the conclusion above becomes clear when we observe that the rejection of the Trinity in verses 4.171 is followed in verses 4.172 by the confirmation that the Messiah and the nearest angels would not scorn to be servants to God. The Qur'an could not have defined the Trinity in one verse as being God, the Messiah, and the nearest angels, and in another as God, Jesus, and Mary. The names mentioned after the Trinity are not meant to be its members.

In verse 5.116, God asks Jesus: "Did you say to people: 'Take me and my mother for two gods besides Allah?'" This may be taken by some to mean that the Trinity is presented as consisting of God, Jesus, and Mary. But, unlike verses 4.171 and 5.73, this verse does not mention the concept of *three*. The Qur'an contains a large number of verses criticizing those who "take gods besides Allah," and most of these verses have nothing to do with Jesus or the concept of the Trinity (e.g. 19.81, 36.74).

Additionally, I think that the Qur'an deliberately ignores naming the members of the Trinity. Verse 4.171 rejects the concept of "three" and verse 5.73 describes that concept as the belief that "Allah is one of three." What is being rejected, therefore, is not the unity of a particular group of three, but the very concept of threesome — that God is three beings, aspects, modes, manifestations, or whatever. The Qur'an focuses on rejecting the concept of the unity of three rather than who those three are. As I have already said, the Qur'an considers the Trinity a form of tritheism, and no playing with words can make the Trinity a form of monotheism.

Verse 5.75 makes the interesting observation that both Jesus and his mother ate food, which is a sign of being human. Having to eat food in order to live is used elsewhere in the Qur'an as a sign that the messengers were ordinary human beings:

> And We did not send before you [O Muhammad!] other than men to whom We gave revelation, so ask the people of the remembrance if you do not know. (21.7) And We did not make them bodies that do not eat food, and they were not immortal. (21.8)
>
> And they (the disbelievers) say: "What is the matter with this Messenger (Muhammad) that he eats food and walks in the markets? Why has an angel not been sent down to him, so that he should have been a warner with him?" (25.7)
>
> And We have not sent before you [O Muhammad!] any messengers but they ate food and walked in the markets. And We have made some of you a test for others: will you have patience? And your Lord is ever seeing. (25.20)

I should stress another important point. A common mistake in studying the Qur'an's discussion of Christian beliefs, including the doctrine of the Trinity, is to suggest that the Qur'an talks about the New Testament only, or simply misunderstands it. The Qur'an rejects particular Christian beliefs, regardless of whether they are found in the New Testament or not. For instance, the Qur'an rejects the worship of Mary, even though Mariolatry is not a New Testament doctrine. The New Testament does not have any special scriptural value outside mainstream Christianity, which was itself defined in the first few centuries after Jesus. The Qur'an is interested in clarifying its positions on doctrines that Christians hold, regardless of the origin of those doctrines.

The Messiah son of Mary was no other than a messenger before whom similar messengers passed away, and his mother was a saintly woman. They used to eat food. See how We make the revelations clear to them, and see how they are deluded!

(Qur'an, 5.75)

9

Jesus: A Man Created by God and a God Created by Humans

In this chapter I will summarize our conclusions about the nature of Jesus. These conclusions are derived by consulting the Qur'an, Jewish and Christian scriptures, and history.

Jesus was a Muslim prophet who was sent, like any other prophet, with the overall objective of guiding people to God's path. He confirmed the verity of Moses' message, including the Torah, and other prophets before him. He tried to reform religious beliefs and practices that had been corrupted over time by unfaithful religious authorities. He was commanded to modify certain aspects of the Mosaic law. He also conveyed the good news about the coming of Muhammad, the last prophet of Islam.

As is the case with all prophets, Jesus was a human being. He never claimed that he possessed any form of divinity. He lived in a Jewish society that was strictly monotheistic and did not tolerate any claim to divinity by anybody other than God. Such claims were considered blasphemous. The concept that Jesus was divine appeared among Gentile converts outside Palestine, probably promoted by Paul who focused on converting Roman pagans to the religion he claimed Jesus preached.

Jesus declared that he was the Messiah which the Jews had been promised. But he stressed that he was a spiritual Messiah and rejected the concept of a military Messiah that the Jews had developed in response to their occupation by foreign forces for centuries. Only a small minority of Jews accepted Jesus' reform of the concept of Messiah, so he had only a smaller number of followers during his life. This is how Paul's missionary efforts with Roman pagans outside Palestine succeeded in replacing Jesus' totally human identity with one that made him divine.

As the Jews did to their Messiah before Jesus, Christians changed the nature of their Messiah, Jesus, after him. But the Jews always believed that the Messiah was a human being, so Christianity's claim that the Messiah was divine is unhistorical.

The attempts to change the image of Jesus from man to god gained more momentum over time. By the time the Gospel of John was written in the late 1st century or early 2nd century, the unhistorical, divine Jesus had already replaced, in many Christian circles, the historical man that Jesus was.

Jesus taught the oneness of God. He realized that he was going to be turned into a god, so he used the expression "son of man" as one way of emphasizing his human nature. Yet ironically, and as irrationally as it may be, this very term was hijacked by those who promoted his divinity and turned it into another way of saying "son of God" in the Christian sense, i.e. as another confirmation of Jesus' divinity.

The concept of "son of God" was itself distorted. Christian theologians have presented this concept as implying some form of divinity. In fact, this Jewish concept never had any divine connotations. The Christian attempts to read the Jewish concept of "sonship of God" as implying divinity is simply an anachronism.

This fundamental change to Jesus' image has resulted in various theological controversies, including how to describe this unique god-man that Jesus was turned into. The edification of Jesus, expressed in the fundamental doctrine of Incarnation, led to the development of the doctrines of Atonement and Trinity. The Atonement was introduced by Paul and became a cornerstone of Christian faith. Yet this most important doctrine is never mentioned or even alluded to in the Gospels. At no point is Jesus quoted as referring to it.

The Trinity was developed centuries after Jesus, yet it also became a fundamental doctrine of Christianity. Anyone who has any doubts about the fact that Christian theologians have substantially changed Jesus' image after him need only learn about how this alien doctrine was developed and incorporated into Christian theology.

To sum up, the Qur'an absolutely rejects Christianity's elevation of Jesus to divinity. It rejects the claims that he was God's son, God ever had offspring, or there is anyone divine other than God. The nature of Jesus' or anyone else's alleged divinity is irrelevant, as the divinity of other than God is rejected without any qualification. The Qur'an presents Jesus as a prophet of Islam, and thus a human being.

The Qur'an states that Jesus taught that he was a human and that he was turned into a god by his followers after him. Significantly, this is what modern scholars have concluded. It is too tempting to see the differences between the Qur'an and Christian sources as one theology view versus another, and many see it or present it so. The reality is that the Qur'an's account of what Jesus was and how he was made god by people is in line with what history tells us. The disagreement, then, is between the Qur'an and history, on one hand, and Christian sources, on the other. Those who choose to believe the latter do not only reject the Qur'an, but they also deny history.

Appendix A

The Qur'anic Verses that Refute Jesus' Divinity

This is a listing of all Qur'anic verses that reject the claim that Jesus was divine. I have not included the many more verses that do not mention Jesus specifically but reject polytheism in general, confirm that God is one, and stress that everyone and everything was created by him. I have also excluded verses that indirectly stress that Jesus was a man, such as those that describe him as a messenger. I have restricted the compilation to those verses that directly reject the deification of Jesus — for instance, by rejecting the doctrine of the Trinity. The verses are listed in their order in the Qur'an.

> The likeness of Jesus in Allah's eye is as the likeness of Adam. He created him of dust, then He said to him "Be!" and he is. (3.59)

> O People of the Book! Commit no excesses in your religion or utter anything concerning Allah but the truth. The Messiah, Jesus son of Mary, was only a messenger of Allah, His Word that He sent to Mary, and a Spirit from Him [that He sent]. So believe in Allah and His messengers, and do not say "Three." Desist, it is better for you! Allah is one God. Far exalted is He above having offspring. His is all that is in the heavens and all that is in the earth. Allah is sufficient a disposer of affairs. (4.171) The Messiah would never scorn to be a servant to Allah, nor would the angels who are nearest to Allah. As for those who scorn His service and are arrogantly proud, He shall gather them all to Himself to answer. (4.172)

> They have indeed disbelieved those who say: "Allah is the Messiah son of Mary." Say [O Muhammad!]: "Who then can do anything against Allah if He had willed to destroy the Messiah son of Mary, his mother, and everyone on earth?" Allah's is the kingdom of the heavens and the earth and all that is between them. He creates what He wills. Allah is able to do all things. (5.17)

> Surely they disbelieve those who say: "Allah is the Messiah son of Mary." The Messiah himself said: "O Children of Israel! Worship Allah, my Lord and your Lord. Whoever joins other gods with Allah, for him Allah has forbidden paradise. His abode is the Fire. The evildoers shall have no helpers." (5.72) Surely they disbelieve those who say: "Allah is one of three." There is only one God. If they will not desist from what they say, a painful torment shall befall the disbelievers among them. (5.73) Will they not rather repent to Allah and seek His forgiveness? Allah is

forgiving, merciful. (5.74) The Messiah son of Mary was no other than a messenger before whom similar messengers passed away, and his mother was a saintly woman. They used to eat food. See how We make the revelations clear to them, and see how they are deluded! (5.75) Say [O Muhammad!]: "Will you worship besides Allah that which has no power to harm or benefit you?" Allah is the Hearer, the Knower. (5.76) Say: "O People of the Book! Commit no excesses of falsehood in your religion, and do not follow the vain desires of folk of old who erred, led many astray, and strayed from the even path. (5.77) Those who disbelieved from among the Children of Israel were cursed by the tongue of David and of Jesus son of Mary. That was because they disobeyed and used to transgress. (5.78)

And when Allah said: "O Jesus son of Mary! Did you say to people: 'Take me and my mother for two gods besides Allah?'" He said: "Glory be to You! I could never say what I have no right to say. If I have said it, then You know it. You know what is in my mind, but I do not know what is in Your mind. You know all unseen things. (5.116) I never said to them anything other than what You commanded me: 'worship Allah, my and your Lord.' I was a witness over them while I was among them, and when You took me You were the watcher over them. You are a witness over all things. (5.117) If You punish them, they are Your servants; and if You forgive them, You are the Invincible, the Wise." (5.118)

The Jews say: "'Uzayr is the son of Allah," and the Christians say: "The Messiah is the son of Allah." That is a saying from their mouths, imitating the saying of the disbelievers of old. May Allah fight them! How deluded they are! (9.30) They have taken their rabbis and monks as lords besides Allah, and so they treated the Messiah son of Mary, although they were not commanded to worship other than One God; there is no God save Him. Far exalted is He above their attribution of partners to Him! (9.31)

He (Jesus) said: "I am Allah's servant. He has given me the Book and has made me a prophet. (19.30) He has made me blessed wherever I may be. He has enjoined upon me prayer and almsgiving so long as I remain alive. (19.31) And [He has made me] kind to my mother and has not made me arrogant or wretched. (19.32) Peace is on me the day I was born, the day I shall die, and the day I shall be raised alive." (19.33) Such was Jesus son of Mary: this is the statement of the truth which they (Christians) dispute. (19.34) Allah would never take offspring [to Himself]. Far exalted is He above this. When He decrees a matter, He says to it only "Be!" and it is. (19.35)

And when the son of Mary was cited as an example, your people [O Muhammad!] turned away from him. (43.57) They said: "Are our gods better, or is he?" They raise this only by way of disputation; they are merely a contentious people. (43.58) He is only a servant on whom We bestowed favor and whom We made an example for the Children of Israel. (43.59)

When Jesus came with clear proofs, he said: "I have come to you with Wisdom, and to make plain some of what you have disagreed on. Keep your duty to Allah, and obey me. (43.63) Allah is my Lord and your Lord. So worship Him. This is a straight way." (43.64)

References

Arabic Gospel of the Infancy, translated by W. Wake, *The Lost Books of the Bible and the Forgotten Books of Eden*, A&B Publishers Group: New York, 1926, 38-59.

Berakoth, *Hebrew-English edition of the Babylonian Talmud*, edited by I. Epstein, Translated by M. Simon, The Soncino Press: London, 1972.

Bock, D. L. (1991), "The Son of Man in Luke 5:24," *Bulletin for Biblical Research*, 1, 109-121.

Bruce, F.F. (1982). "The Background to the Son of Man Sayings." In: H. H. Rowdon (ed.), *Christ The Lord: Studies in Christology presented to Donald Guthrie*, Inter-Varsity Press: Leicester, 50-70.

Campbell, J. Y. (1947). "The Origin and Meaning of the Term Son of Man," *Journal of Theological Studies*, 48, 145-155.

Cragg, K. (1999). *Jesus and the Muslim*, Oneworld Publications: Oxford.

Dawud, A. A. (1994). *Muhammad in the Bible*, The Ministry of Awqaf and Islamic Affairs: Qatar.

Dunn, J. (2003). *Jesus Remembered: Christianity in the Making, vol. 1*, Wm. B. Eerdmans Publishing Company: Michigan.

Ehrman, B. (2007). *Misquoting Jesus: The Story Behind Who Changed the Bible and Why*, HarperSanFrancisco: New York.

Elliot, J. H. (2007). "Jesus the Israelite was Neither a 'Jew' nor a 'Christian': On Correcting Misleading Nomenclature," *Journal for the Study of the Historical Jesus*, 5, 119-154.

Fatoohi, L. (2007). *The Mystery of the Historical Jesus: The Messiah in the Qur'an, the Bible, and Historical Sources*, Luna Plena Publishing: UK.

Fatoohi, L. (2008a). *The Mystery of the Crucifixion: The Attempt to Kill Jesus in the Qur'an, the New Testament, and Historical Sources*, Luna Plena Publishing: UK.

Fatoohi, L. (2008b). *The Mystery of Israel in Ancient Egypt: The Exodus in the Qur'an, the Old Testament, Archaeological Finds, and Historical Sources*, Luna Plena Publishing: UK.

Fatoohi, L. (2009). *The Mystery of the Messiah: Jesus' Messiahship in the Qur'an, the New Testament, the Old Testament, and other Jewish Sources*, Luna Plena Publishing: UK.

Hick, J. (1997). "Islam and Christian Monotheism." In: D. Cohn-Sherbok (ed.), *Islam in a World of Diverse Faiths*, Palgrave Macmillan: New York, 1-17.

Horbury, W. (1985). "The Messianic Associations of the 'Son of Man'," *Journal of Theological Studies*, 36, 34-55.

Hurtado, L. (2003). "Homage to the Historical Jesus and Early Christian Devotion," *Journal for the Study of the Historical Jesus*, 1, 131-146.

Kazen, T. (2007). "The Coming Son of Man Revisited," *Journal for the Study of the Historical Jesus*, 5, 155-174.

Kelly, J. N. D. (1999). *Early Christian Creeds (3rd Edition)*, Longman: England.

Longenecker, R. N. (1969). "'Son of Man' as a Self-Designation of Jesus," *Journal of the Evangelical Theological Society*, 12, 151-158.

Longenecker, R. N. (1975), "'Son of Man' Imagery: Some Implications for Theology and Discipleship," *Journal of the Evangelical Theological Society*, 18, 3-16.

Miller, R. J. (2003). *Born Divine: The Births of Jesus and Other Sons of God*, Polebridge Press: California.

Parrinder, G. (1995). *Jesus in the Qur'an*, Oneworld Publications: Oxford.

Sanders, E. P. (1995). *The Historical Figure of Jesus*, Penguin Books: England.

Sanhedrin, *Hebrew-English edition of the Babylonian Talmud*, edited by I. Epstein, Translated by J. Shachter & H. Freedman, The Soncino Press: London, 1969.

Ta'anith, *Hebrew-English edition of the Babylonian Talmud*, edited by I. Epstein, Translated by J. Rabbinowitz, The Soncino Press: London, 1984.

Theissen, G. & Merz, A. (1999). *The Historical Jesus: A Comprehensive Guide*, SCM Press: London.

Vermes, G. (2000). *The Changing Faces of Jesus*, Penguin Books: London.

Vermes, G. (2005). *The Passion*, Penguin Books: London.

Witmer, J. A. (1998). *Immanuel: Jesus Christ, Cornerstone of our Faith*, Word Publishing: Tennessee.

Index of Qur'anic Verses

Verse	Page(s)
2.13	67
2.111	66
2.112	66
2.116	59
2.117	48
2.127-128	23
2.130	10
2.131	10
2.132	10
2.133	10
2.136	13
2.253	14, 57
2.285	12
2.34	46
2.62	11, 66
2.67	69
2.80	69
2.87	16
2.92	69
3.28	69
3.46	70
3.49	16
3.50	23
3.52	13
3.59	19, 111
3.64	68
3.80	64
3.83	57
3.84	12
4.48	58
4.64	15
4.89	69
4.116	58
4.125	69
4.153	69
4.163	11, 12
4.164	11
4.171	103, 104, 111
4.172	6, 103, 104, 111
5.17	57, 65, 111
5.18	65, 66
5.44	10
5.66	24
5.69	66
5.72	103, 111
5.72-75	104
5.73	103, 104, 111
5.74	103, 112
5.75	16, 103, 104, 112
5.76	103, 112
5.77	103, 112
5.78	103, 112
5.110	70
5.111	13
5.116	70, 71, 104, 112
5.117	70, 112
5.118	70, 112
6.61	15
6.100	62
6.101	62, 65
6.102	57
6.103	57, 59
7.11	46
7.12	61
7.37	15
7.67	15
7.148	69
7.152	69
7.157	24
7.180	59
9.30	67, 112
9.31	67, 68, 112
9.34	68
10.68	60
10.72	10
11.27	16
11.69-83	15
12.109	16
13.33	59
14.10	17
14.11	17
14.30	59
15.27	61
15.51-74	15
16.49	62
16.51	69

16.57	60	25.2	63
16.58	60	25.7	105
16.59	60	25.20	105
17.40	61	26.154	17
17.55	13	26.186	17
17.61	46	29.31-34	15
17.94	17	30.20	19
17.95	17	33.7	12
17.110	59	33.40	11, 25
17.111	63, 69	34.40	61
18.4	63	34.41	61
18.4-5	59	35.1	15
18.15	69	36.74	104
18.50	46	37.35	96
19.30	8, 12, 13, 18, 63, 112	37.149	61
		37.150	61
19.31	18, 63, 112	37.151	61
19.32	63, 112	37.152	61, 65
19.33	63, 112	37.153	61
19.34	63, 112	37.154	61
19.34-35	64	37.155	61
19.35	63, 69, 112	37.156	61
19.81	69, 104	37.157	61
19.88	63	38.76	61
19.89	63	39.2	59
19.90	63	39.3	59
19.91	63	39.4	62, 69
19.92	63, 69	42.11	57
19.93	63	42.13	11
20.8	59	43.16	60
20.47	23	43.17	60
20.116	46	43.19	61
21.3	17	43.20	61
21.7	105	43.57	64, 112
21.8	105	43.58	64, 112
21.21	69	43.59	64, 112
21.24	69	43.63	19, 64
21.26	63	43.64	19, 64
21.27	63	43.65	64
21.28	63	43.80	15
21.29	63	43.81	62
22.5	19	43.82	62
22.26-27	23	46.9	11
22.78	9, 25	47.19	57, 96
23.24	17	48.29	96
23.47	17	52.39	60
23.84-92	59	53.18	60

53.19	60	57.3	57
53.20	60	57.27	16
53.21	60	59.22-24	59
53.21-22	60	59.24	59
53.22	60	61.6	24
53.27	61	72.3	62, 65
53.28	61	81.8-9	60
53.32	67	112.1	63
54.23	17	112.2	63
54.24	17	112.3	63, 65
54.25	17	112.4	63
55.15	61		

Index of Biblical Passages

Reference	Page
Gen. 6:1-4	35
Gen. 18:10-11	90
Exo. 4:22-23	36
Exo. 40:12-15	29
Lev. 24:10-16	54
Deut. 18:15	21
1 Sam. 10:1	29
1 Sam. 16:12-13	90
2 Sam. 7:14	35
2 Sam. 23:3	90
1 Kings 19:15-16	29
1 Chr. 16:15-22	29
Job 1:6	35
Job 2:1	35
Job 38:7	35
Ps. 2:7	35, 49
Ps. 29:1	35
Ps. 82:1-7	55
Ps. 82:7	55
Ps. 89:6	35
Isa. 7:14	51
Isa. 61:1	29
Dan. 7:13	73, 74, 76, 77
Dan. 7:13-14	74
Dan. 8:17	74
Hos. 11:1	35
Matt. 1:18	51
Matt. 1:20	51
Matt. 1:23	51
Matt. 2:11	51
Matt. 2:15	51
Matt. 3:17	41, 51
Matt. 4:3	52
Matt. 4:6	52
Matt. 5:9	40
Matt. 5:16	40
Matt. 5:17-20	24
Matt. 8:20	80
Matt. 8:29	52
Matt. 9:6	77
Matt. 10:24-25	18
Matt. 10:32	80
Matt. 10:32-33	42
Matt. 10:33	80
Matt. 10:40-41	21
Matt. 11:18	80
Matt. 11:27	41, 43
Matt. 12:17-18	3, 18
Matt. 13:41	77
Matt. 13:55-58	20
Matt. 14:24-33	39
Matt. 14:33	53
Matt. 16:13	80
Matt. 16:13-14	22
Matt. 16:13-16	82
Matt. 16:16	39
Matt. 16:21	93
Matt. 16:27	76
Matt. 17:1-5	51
Matt. 17:5	41
Matt. 17:12	93
Matt. 18:11	78
Matt. 20:28	80
Matt. 21:10-11	22
Matt. 21:46	22
Matt. 22:21	81
Matt. 24:30	76
Matt. 25:31	76
Matt. 26:25	23
Matt. 26:63	52
Matt. 26:63-65	53
Matt. 26:64	76
Matt. 27:40	53
Matt. 27:54	53
Mark 1:1	52
Mark 1:10-11	49
Mark 1:11	41
Mark 2:10	80
Mark 2:10-12	77
Mark 3:11	52
Mark 5:7	52
Mark 6:2-5	3, 21
Mark 6:3	72
Mark 6:14-15	22
Mark 6:47-51	39
Mark 8:27	80

Index of Biblical Passages

Passage	Pages
Mark 8:27-28	22
Mark 8:27-29	82
Mark 8:29	39, 81
Mark 8:31	93
Mark 8:38	77, 79, 80
Mark 9:2-8	50
Mark 9:5	3, 23
Mark 9:7	41
Mark 9:12	93
Mark 10:45	80
Mark 11:25	40
Mark 12:17	81
Mark 13:26	76
Mark 13:32	41
Mark 14:61	81
Mark 14:61-64	54
Mark 14:62	76
Mark 15:39	53
Luke 1:13-19	90
Luke 1:32	50
Luke 1:35	50
Luke 3:21-22	50
Luke 3:22	41, 50
Luke 3:38	40
Luke 4:3	52
Luke 4:9	52
Luke 4:22-24	20
Luke 4:41	53
Luke 5:24	77
Luke 6:35	40
Luke 6:35-36	40
Luke 7:14-16	22
Luke 7:39	22
Luke 8:28	52
Luke 9:7-8	22
Luke 9:18	80
Luke 9:18-19	22
Luke 9:22	93
Luke 9:26	76, 80
Luke 9:35	41
Luke 10:22	41, 43
Luke 12:8	76, 80
Luke 12:32	40
Luke 13:31-34	21
Luke 17:25	93
Luke 20:25	81
Luke 21:27	76
Luke 22:15	93
Luke 22:27	80
Luke 22:70-71	53
Luke 24:26	93
Luke 24:46	93
John 1:1-2	45
John 1:9-11	47
John 1:14	41, 45
John 1:15	46
John 1:49	52
John 1:51	77
John 3:13	77
John 3:14-16	77
John 3:16	41
John 3:18	41
John 4:17-19	22
John 4:44	20
John 5:16-18	42, 53
John 5:21-30	44
John 5:26-27	77
John 6:12-14	22
John 6:27	77
John 6:40	43
John 6:62	77
John 7:39-40	22
John 7:50-52	22
John 8:31	40
John 8:41	40
John 8:42-44	40
John 8:58-59	45
John 9:16-17	22
John 10:17-18	43
John 10:30	3, 44
John 10:32-36	53, 55
John 10:36	83
John 10:38	44
John 11:4	53
John 11:27	52, 53
John 12:34	78
John 12:49	47
John 13:1-3	47
John 14:6	42
John 14:7-11	44
John 14:28	47
John 14:31	47
John 16:27-28	47
John 17:5	45

John 17:11	44	Rom. 9:4	40
John 17:24	45	Rom. 9:5	45, 49
John 19:7	54	1 Cor. 7:18-19	91
John 20:17	40	1 Cor. 15:17	92
John 20:21	47	1 Cor. 15:22	92
John 20:27-28	44	1 Cor. 15:45-50	19
John 20:30-31	53	1 Cor. 15.47	45, 49
John 20:31	52	2 Cor. 11:4-6	87
Acts 3:13	18	Gal. 1:11-12	88
Acts 3:20-22	21	Eph. 2:15	93
Acts 3:26	18	Phi. 2:5-11	49
Acts 4:27	18	Phi. 2:5-8	19
Acts 4:30	18	Phi. 2:6	3, 45
Acts 7:56	78	Col. 1:15	46
Acts 9:3-8	88	Col. 1:16	46
Acts 9:20	53	Tit. 2:13	45
Acts 10:37-38	50	Heb. 1:2	48
Acts 13:32-33	49	Heb. 1:5	42
Acts 15:29	91	Heb. 2:6	78
Acts 22:6-10	88	1 John 2:29	40
Acts 26:13-18	88	1 John 3:9	40
Rom. 1:3	20, 45, 49	1 John 4:9	41
Rom. 1:3-4	49	1 John 5:1	40
Rom. 2:25-29	91	1 John 5:11-13	42
Rom. 3:21-26	92	1 John 5:18	40
Rom. 3:29-30	91	Rev. 1:13	78
Rom. 5:6-21	92	Rev. 14:14	76, 78

Index of Names and Subjects

Aaron (prophet), 10, 11, 17, 25, 30, 92
Abraham (prophet), 9-12, 15, 16, 18, 23, 45, 69, 89, 92
Adam (prophet), 3, 10, 12, 19, 20, 40, 45, 46, 73, 92, 93, 111
adoptionism, 48, 68, 69, 99
Alexander (Bishop), 100
Alexander the Great, 89
Antioch, 91
apocrypha, 3, 36, 39, 53, 97, 99
Apollo (god), 89
Apollonius of Tyana, 89
Arabia, 16, 25, 57, 59-61, 63, 67
Arianism, 100
Arius, 100
Assyrians, 91
atonement, 121
Augustine, 93
Augustus (emperor), 89
Babylon, 29
Babylonians, 29, 91
Barnabas, 91
Chalcedon Council, 102
Constantine (emperor), 100
Constantinople Council, 101
Constantinople, 102
crucifixion, 120, 121
Cyrus (king), 29
Damascus, 88
David (prophet), 10-13, 20, 30, 31, 35, 45, 49, 103, 112
Day of Judgment, 15, 68
Day of Resurrection, 12, 31, 43, 61
Dead Sea Scrolls, 30
Docetism, 4, 99
Easter, 52, 71, 80
Egypt, 123
Emmanuel, 51

English Standard Version Bible, 6
Ezra (prophet), 67, 73-75
Gabriel, 14, 50
Galilee, 22
Hanina ben Dosa, 37
Heracles (god), 89
Heraclitus, 47
Herod Antipas (king), 18, 21, 22
Herod the Great (king), 75
Honi, 37
Hūd (prophet), 15
Iblīs (Satan), 46
Immaculate Conception, 102
Incarnation, 3, 47-49, 68, 92, 99, 102
Injīl (Jesus' Book), 9, 23, 24
Iraq, 3
Isaac (prophet), 10-12, 18
Isaiah (prophet), 18, 51
Ishmael (prophet), 10-12
Jacob (prophet), 10-12, 18, 92, 124
Jerusalem, 21, 22, 29, 78, 91
Job (prophet), 11
John (prophet), 12
Jonah (prophet), 11
Joseph (prophet), 10, 11
Judas Iscariot, 47
Judea (kingdom), 75, 91
Judea, 51
King James Version Bible, 6
Lazarus, 52, 53
Lot (prophet), 15
Maimonides, 75
Mariolatry, 71, 102, 105
Modalism, 100
monotheism, 4, 59, 99, 100, 103, 104
Moses (prophet), 9-12, 15-17, 21, 23-25, 30, 35, 36, 50, 54, 69, 77, 91, 92, 107

Nazareth, 21, 22
Nebuchadnezzar II (king), 29, 75
Nicea Council, 100
Noah (prophet), 9, 10-12, 16
original sin, 102
Palestine, 79
Passover, 47
patripassionism, 100
Peter (disciple), 18, 21, 39, 50, 81, 82
Pharaoh, 36
Philo, 47, 48
Pilate (Pontius), 18, 101
Pius IX (Pope), 102
Pius XII (Pope), 102
Plato, 89
Pythagoras, 89
Romans, 75, 122
Rome, 78
Sabaeans, 10, 66
Sabbath, 37
Sabellianism, 100
Sabellius, 100
Ṣāliḥ (prophet), 17
Sanhedrin, 18, 81, 116
Satan, 35, 46
Shuʻayb (prophet), 17
Solomon (prophet), 10-12, 36
Talmud, 37, 115, 116
Tertullian, 100
Thomas (disciple), 44
Torah, 9, 10, 23, 24, 107
tritheism, 100, 103, 104
Zechariah (prophet), 10, 12, 89
Zedekiah (king), 75
Zeus (god), 89

The Mystery of the Messiah
The Messiahship of Jesus in the Qur'an, New Testament, Old Testament, and Other Sources

• The Messiah in Judaism, Christianity, and Islam

• An Islamic reading of the history of the concept of "Messiah"

• Unhistorical images of the Jewish and Christian Messiahs

• The misrepresentation of the Messiah as king

• The second coming of the Christian Messiah

Publication Date: May 2009
ISBN: 978-1-906342-05-0
Available from Amazon and other bookstores

The Messiah is the central figure of the largest religion in the world, as Christianity was formed around Jesus' messiahship. Judaism also gives the Messiah a special and high position, although it denies that Jesus was the Messiah, so the Jews continue to wait for the coming of their Messiah.

The Qur'an confirms the Christian belief that Jesus was the Messiah, but it has fundamental differences with the Christian representation of the Messiah. Islam has even more differences with the Jewish concept of the Messiah.

This book compares the concept of "Messiah" in Judaism, Christianity, and Islam. It examines the portrayal of the Messiah in the Old Testament and other Jewish writings, the New Testament, and the Qur'an. It develops a complete picture of how this concept appeared, what it originally represented, and how it was changed over time by different believers. The study shows why and how the Messiah was developed in Judaism into a military king whose main role is to re-establish Israel and restore its glory. It also explains how Christianity turned this victorious Jewish warrior into a suffering spiritual king.

The author's ultimate goal is to show that the Qur'anic Messiah is the historical one. Neither a victorious royal with a political agenda nor a defeated spiritual teacher who ended up on the cross, the Messiah was a prophet sent by God. This new critical reading of the history of the "Messiah" challenges deep-rooted prejudices and misunderstandings about this concept.

The Mystery of the Crucifixion
The Attempt to Kill Jesus in the Qur'an, the New Testament, and Historical Sources

• Flaws of the Gospel accounts of the crucifixion

• Does history really support the crucifixion tradition?

• The Qur'an's explanation of the crucifixion

• The origin of the theology of the cross

• The reality of Jesus' appearances after the crucifixion

Publication Date: November 2008
ISBN: 978-1-906342-04-3
Available from Amazon and other bookstores

Numerous books and articles have been published about the crucifixion. Western studies have focused on the Christian narratives and historical sources, but most of them have completely ignored the Qur'an, which denies that Jesus was crucified. Muslim scholars have also studied the Qur'an's account but mostly in exegetical works that focused on the Qur'an's version of the story, with some comparative references to the Gospel narratives but almost no consideration of historical sources.

This book takes a new approach by considering the crucifixion in the Qur'an, Christian writings, and early historical sources. It discusses the serious flaws in the Gospel accounts and the unreliability of the few non-scriptural sources. The book also challenges common modern alternative readings of the history of that event. One new contribution that this study makes to the literature of the crucifixion is its new interpretation of all related Qur'anic verses. It also presents a coherent explanation of the development of the fictitious story of the crucifixion of Jesus.

The theology of the cross that Paul developed is also examined. The book shows that the doctrine of the atonement conflicts with the Gospel teachings and is refuted in the Qur'an.

The Mystery of the Historical Jesus
The Messiah in the Qur'an, the Bible, and Historical Sources

- Jesus in the Qur'an, Christian writings, and historical sources
- The scriptural Jesus in the light of history
- The life and teachings of the historical Jesus
- The time and places in which Jesus lived
- Jesus and the Jews and the Romans
- The historical Jesus versus the theological one

Publication Date: September 2007
ISBN: 978-1-906342-01-2
Available from Amazon and other bookstores

In the two millennia since his birth, countless writers have published numerous books and articles on every aspect of Jesus' life, personality, teachings, and environment. Depending on the backgrounds, goals, and trainings of their respective authors, these works relied on the New Testament, other Christian sources, Jewish writings, or other historical sources, or on combinations of these writings. The Qur'an is rarely mentioned, let alone seriously considered, by the mainly Christian authors of these studies. This explicit or implicit neglect reflects a presumed historical worthlessness of the Qur'an.

Muslim scholars have also written extensively about Jesus. Contrary to their Western counterparts, they have studied in detail what the Qur'an and other Islamic sources say about Jesus. The Christian image of Jesus is often cited to be dismissed, usually on the basis of what Islamic sources say, but at times also because of its incoherence and inconsistency. While Western scholars have ignored the Qur'an, Muslim writers have shown no interest in independent historical sources.

This book fills a gap in the literature on the historical Jesus by taking the unique approach of considering together the Qur'an, the Gospels, and other religious and historical sources. This genuinely new contribution to the scholarship on the historical Jesus shows that, unlike the New Testament accounts, the Qur'anic image of Jesus is both internally consistent and reconcilable with known history. While showing that our understanding of how the New Testament was formed and our growing knowledge of history confirm that the Christian Jesus is unhistorical, this study makes a strong case for the historicity of the Jesus of the Qur'an.

The Mystery of Israel in Ancient Egypt
The Exodus in the Qur'an, the Old Testament, Archaeological Finds, and Historical Sources

- The Israelites in ancient Egypt
- The Qur'anic and Biblical accounts of the exodus
- Historical problems in the Biblical narrative
- The exodus in archaeological finds
- The exodus in historical sources
- Identifying the Pharaoh of the exodus

Publication Date: December 2008
ISBN: 978-1-906342-03-6
Available from Amazon and other bookstores

    Few events in history have fascinated the layperson and the scholar as much as the exodus of the Israelites from ancient Egypt. This phenomenal interest has led to extensive research into scriptural, historical, and archaeological sources. The Qur'an, however, has been completely ignored by Western researchers because of the faith put in the Biblical narrative and the prejudiced view that the Qur'an's account is based on Jewish sources, including the Bible.
    This book examines in detail the Biblical narrative of the exodus, showing that it contains a substantial amount of inaccurate and false information. It also shows that the similarities between the Qur'anic exodus and its Biblical counterpart are very limited and the differences between the two scriptures are much greater in number and detail. Particularly significant is the fact that the Qur'an is free of the erroneous and inaccurate Biblical statements that have contributed to the rejection of the historicity of the exodus by many scholars. The book demonstrates that the Qur'anic account is consistent with what we know today from archaeological finds and historical sources. This pioneering study is an attempt to create what might be called "Qur'anic archaeology."

The Prophet Joseph in the Qur'an, the Bible, and History
A new, detailed commentary on the Qur'anic Chapter of Joseph

- Modern and comprehensive interpretation of the sūra of Joseph

- Verse by verse analysis and commentary

- Comparative references to classical interpretations

- Comparison between the story in the Qur'an and its Biblical counterpart

- Examination of the historical time and place where Joseph lived

- Explanation of the Qur'an's style in relating history

Publication Date: August 2007
ISBN: 978-1-906342-00-5
Available from Amazon and other bookstores

    The Qur'anic sūra (chapter) of Joseph deals almost entirely with the story of this noble Prophet, his brothers, and their father Prophet Jacob. Since the revelation of the Qur'an fourteen centuries ago, there have been numerous attempts to interpret this sūra. The present study is a genuinely new look at the sūra — including careful examination of the historical background of its story and detailed comparison with the corresponding Biblical narrative. While referring to interpretations from classical exegetical works, this book offers new insights into the meanings and magnificence of this Qur'anic text.

    The author is not only concerned with analyzing the individual verses; he is equally focused on showing how various verses are interrelated, explicitly and subtly, to form a unique textual unit. He shows particular interest in unveiling subtle references and meanings that are often overlooked or missed by exegetes. Through this comprehensive study, the author elucidates why the Qur'an has always been firmly believed to be a unique book that could have only been inspired by Allah.

www.ingramcontent.com/pod-product-compliance
Lightning Source LLC
Chambersburg PA
CBHW031553040426
42452CB00006B/295